CONTEMPORARY ENGLISH POETRY
An Introduction

CONTEMPORARY
ENGLISH POETRY

An Introduction

BY
ANTHONY THWAITE

HEINEMANN

MELBOURNE LONDON TORONTO

1959

FIRST PUBLISHED 1959

PR
601
T5

PUBLISHED BY
WILLIAM HEINEMANN LTD
15–16 QUEEN STREET, LONDON, W.I
PRINTED IN GREAT BRITAIN BY
MORRISON AND GIBB LTD, LONDON AND EDINBURGH

Contents

dv

r

Author's Note

The original version of this book was published in May 1957 by Kenkyusha Ltd., Tokyo, under the title *Essays on Contemporary English Poetry*. It was based on lectures I had given to students of English literature at Tokyo University and elsewhere in Japan, and I wrote it because I felt there was a need for a book on the subject which would be clear yet sufficiently detailed. I felt then, as I do now, that the only book which came anywhere near covering the ground in a reasonable, informative, critical way was G. S. Fraser's *The Modern Writer and his World*; yet even that admirable book has its drawbacks, because the chapter on poetry is only one among four others, and thus many names and much information are crammed into a comparatively small space.

My book has apparently been found to be useful by students, and even lecturers, in Japan. But when I came to thinking of revising it for an English-speaking audience, there was obviously a good deal to be done. The original version was written specifically with a Japanese audience in mind, with peculiar difficulties about vocabulary, background, and where to look for the poems and criticism with which the book deals. Several English friends, both here and in Japan, saw a place for it as an introduction for the sixth form and general reader, but obviously this new audience would not need such expressions as 'dead letter' or 'maiden name' explained to it, nor would it need a page reference in the notes for every quotation. The original introductory chapter was implicitly designed to calm the special fears of Japanese students about English poetry. There were several deliberate omissions, for one reason and another. And so on.

I have therefore written an entirely new introductory chapter, though it incorporates some of my old material; I have added a chapter on Wilfred Owen and D. H. Lawrence, and have brought three or four new poets into the scheme of the last chapter; and I have made as close and careful a revision as I can of the rest, weeding out those explanations which might annoy rather than illuminate. I have also cut out the Notes, and brought the Select Bibliography up to date.

Almost every poem to which I refer in any detail can be found in one or other of the following books: the Penguin *Gerard Manley Hopkins*, the Penguin *Contemporary Verse*, and *New Lines* (published by Macmillan, edited by Robert Conquest). Indeed, the book is intended to be used alongside these, so that the reader is never far from the poem, in the desert of unrelated criticism.

ANTHONY THWAITE

CHAPTER ONE

The General Scene

Contemporary poetry—the poetry which is peculiarly that of today and no other—did not begin at any particular time or with any particular poet. The word 'contemporary' has itself grown to be a useful blanket term with which to cover many different products of man's activity today—poetry, fiction, painting, sculpture, philosophy, music, architecture, furniture, wallpaper, kitchen utensils. In the domestic articles, 'contemporary' refers to design: this wallpaper could not have been designed by William Morris, nor that teapot by Josiah Wedgwood; and their line and colour and general look are opposed, when we use the word, to 'traditional' or 'period' wallpaper and teapots.

In fields such as poetry, philosophy and music, however, much more than design is meant. By choice, a wall-paper designer can make a 'contemporary' or a 'traditional' wall-paper. But a philosopher cannot wilfully construct a 'traditional' philosophy, or a poet a 'traditional' poem: however much of a pastiche the finished product may be, it is still modified and perhaps, however subtly and unconsciously, determined by the time at which it was written. This is not to say that we cannot sometimes usefully use the word 'traditional' of some poets or poems today; Edmund Blunden, Herbert Palmer, Roy Campbell, Andrew Young, Edwin Muir—to take only a few of the better-known figures—have all, in their different ways, written poems that can be called 'traditional'; but not in the sense of a twentieth century craftsman imitating, closely and deliberately, the style of a

Wedgwood teapot; rather, these men have sometimes adopted the form or the imagery, or sometimes both, of an earlier time, and when I say 'adopted' I do not mean that they have necessarily consciously chosen to do this. A poet is not, or should not be, a man who, when he sits down to write, says to himself, 'I shall write about the spirit of the age'; nor should he throw in the sponge and say, 'I hate the modern world; I shall write like Herbert' (or Clare, or Byron, or any other safely buried poet). He should not set out to write either a 'modern' or a 'traditional' poem, a poem which is 'Classical' or a poem which is 'Romantic'. A poem begins, not in attitudes, but in words; and—unless we are recluses or impregnable pedants—the words of our usual speech (which filter through into poems) are the words of our day.

At the beginning of this century—a convenient and nicely-rounded date, one might have thought, for something new— the most influential figure in the poetry of our time, T. S. Eliot, had not even started to write the work which has given him that influence—he was, after all, only 12 and, one imagines, had not yet even discovered his first love in poetry: Shelley. Alfred Austin was the official, and Kipling the un-official, laureate of Great Britain. Swinburne, Wilde, Dowson, Symons were the 'contemporary' poets; they reflected, at least, some part of the literary spirit of the age, and were labelled or parodied as 'fleshly' (Swinburne) or 'decadent' and 'greenery-yallery' (Wilde, Dowson, Symons). Yeats, by association, was one of these, and if he had died in 1900— at the age of 35—he would no doubt now be considered an insubstantial and delicate minor poet. Hopkins had died in 1889, but very little of his poetry had been published, and few knew of him. The one reputation which was just begin-ning to grow, and which still survives practically undimin-ished today, was that of Housman: *A Shropshire Lad* was published in 1896, and the South African War soon after made its mixture of pride and gloom, pessimism and nostalgia, extremely popular.

New poetry often has to fight its battles, even with those whose inclination and training have led them to appreciate poetry of earlier periods than their own. Look, for instance, at this passage from a review of Keats's *Endymion*, published in the *Quarterly Review* in 1818:

> This author is a copyist of Leigh Hunt; but he is more un-intelligible, almost as rugged, twice as diffuse, and ten times more tiresome and absurd than his prototype . . . he more than rivals the insanity of [Leigh Hunt's] poetry.

Or look at this review, written by Hazlitt—one of the two great Romantic critics—and published in 1816 in the *Edinburgh Review*. Hazlitt was writing about the recent appearance of Coleridge's *Kubla Khan*, which few nowadays would question as one of the best-known and best-loved poems in the English language:

> Upon the whole, we look upon this publication as one of the most notable pieces of impertinence of which the press has lately been made guilty; and one of the boldest experiments that has yet been made on the patience or understanding of the public. The thing now before us is utterly destitute of value. It exhibits from beginning to end not a ray of genius . . . raving . . . drivelling . . . nonsense.

The opinion expressed there is strangely similar to that in the review which Sir John Squire published in *The London Mercury* when Eliot's *The Waste Land* first appeared, a little over a hundred years after Hazlitt's review. Squire, it is true, was more urbane and jocular in his tone than Hazlitt—but that merely reflects a change in the manners of literary journalism. The impertinence of foisting nonsense on to a gullible and defenceless public—that has been the common charge.

There has been, for about forty years now, a popular idea of what contemporary poetry is like; if one were to believe the gibes of journalists, it has all been written in uneven lines, without rhyme, capital letters or syntax, and has been concerned with obscure and inflated references to sewage, drains and death. All this without any honesty on the part of the poets; all of them have been charlatans. The idea still goes on. A leading weekly periodical recently set a competition on 'Cynical Definitions'. and the entries for poetry (which most competitors took to be modern poetry) were of this type:

> *Rhyme:* a primitive form of jingle, now abandoned in poetry.
> *Meaning:* the conveyance of precise ideas by means of language, now abandoned in poetry.
> *Metre:* something that went out with Lord Tennyson.
> *Communication:* non-existent problem since 1914.
> *Obscure:* profound.
> *Afflatus:* wind, an essential component of modern poetry.

Just how irrelevant (and therefore unfunny) these definitions are can be seen if one looks at, say, a recent volume of the annual anthology *New Poems*, issued by the P.E.N. Club. Other charges could be made against some of the poems—of tameness, for example—but few or none of obscurity or lack of attention to form.

How, then, did the charges begin? Leaving aside the general undercurrent of art-hatred or art-despising which has been characteristic of the English since the time of the Commonwealth, there *was* a break in the tradition of English verse some time during the first ten or fifteen years of the twentieth century; not the first break, of course, but the first important one since the beginning of that movement in the eighteenth century which is generally called Romantic. The first cracks in the break perhaps started in France; but as far as English poetry is concerned, the revolutionaries were mainly Americans: Ezra Pound, Amy Lowell, H. D. (Hilda Doolittle), and a little later Eliot and E. E. Cummings. The first three were at the centre of the Imagist movement. In 1915, the Imagist manifesto was issued; in it, three main resolutions were made:

(1) To use the language of common speech, but to employ always the exact word, not the nearly exact, nor the merely decorative word.
(2) To produce poetry that is hard and clear, and not to deal in vague generalities, however magnificent and sonorous.
(3) To create new rhythms and not to copy old rhythms, which merely echo old moods.

The effect of this, on the poets who subscribed to it, was to cut language and imagery to the bone. The poems of the Imagists seem to try to capture a momentary observation, rather in the way that a Japanese *haiku* does, though without the *haiku's* veils of suggestion. This—a complete poem by Pound—is a fair example:

> The apparition of these faces in the crowd:
> Petals on a wet, black bough.

The essence, ideally, was compression, compression of the most drastic sort. But in the weaker poems written in this manner and on these assumptions, such as some of those by H. D., compression and hard objectivity on the one hand and what one might call the traditional poem's narrative thread on the other, seem to be working in opposition; and the poem becomes dull and even confused.

There were other areas of revolt: the anthology *Wheels*, for example, which was mainly a platform for the Sitwell family, particularly Edith. And in 1923—the year after the publication of *The Waste Land*—there was practically a riot at the Aeolian Hall in London, where Edith Sitwell first read her sequence *Façade* through a megaphone concealed behind a giant mask-backcloth, to the accompaniment of William Walton's music. But I shall mention little more than this about the Sitwell family and its contribution to English poetry. Someone has said that the Sitwells belong more to the history of publicity than that of poetry, and I think there may well be something in this; though to many people 'modern poetry' means Edith Sitwell, and though to several others—whose tastes I often share—she is one of the leading poets of the century.

But neither the Imagists, nor *The Waste Land*, nor even the irrepressible Sitwells, really penetrated English life as 'the modern poets' yet awhile. The anthologies of *Georgian Poetry*, edited by Sir Edward Marsh and issued between 1912 and 1920; the work of G. K. Chesterton, John Drinkwater, John Masefield and J. C. Squire; the anthologies for schools edited by Squire—this was what the poetry-reading public of the First World War and the 1920s was mainly fed on, and it is disturbing to know that in many schools even today this sort of stuff (particularly the Squire anthologies) is *still* put across as representative modern verse. It is difficult to characterise the sort of poetry which appeared in these books, since Robert Graves and D. H. Lawrence, for example, were included in some volumes of *Georgian Poetry*, and even Eliot managed to make a single fugitive appearance in one of Squire's school anthologies (though with the most innocuous of his poems which Squire could find, no doubt—'La Figlia Che

Piange'). Broadly, however, it was a kind of rural verse; the country, and its animals, birds, flowers, yokels and pubs, seen by townsmen. There was a good deal of praise of beer and cricket; and Squire even wrote an extraordinarily dull long poem about a rugger match. England and Englishness were heavily supported, but it was Olde Englande and Olde Englishnesse; industry was frowned on, and a number of poems were written about blades of grass undermining factory chimneys.

Out of all this, a few good poems survive; some of Edmund Blunden's, for example, have a real strength and honest simplicity of their own. But the manner in general was a cul-de-sac, a running backwards into areas of experience which will always have a place in the English tradition (in Edward Thomas, Andrew Young, R. S. Thomas and Blunden, for example, to take good poets of four different modern generations), but which really lie off the main road. The peculiar difficulties and complexities of modern life demanded new treatment in literature; and Eliot showed, in his essay on the Metaphysical poets (1921), why the treatment would be difficult:

> We can only say that it appears likely that poets in our civilization, as it exists at present, must be *difficult*. Our civilization comprehends great variety and complexity, and that variety and complexity, playing upon a refined sensibility, must produce various and complex results. The poet must become more and more comprehensive, more allusive, more indirect, in order to force, to dislocate if necessary, language into his meaning.

One result of this 'dislocation' was that poetry, in trying to assimilate the fragments in all their complexity, itself became fragmentary. So we got works like *The Waste Land* and Ezra Pound's *Cantos* (the first parts of which were published in 1925), monumental mosaics of fragments, which reflect both tremendous change *and* a tremendous awareness of tradition, of the historical process exemplified in the chaos. In Eliot's own words towards the end of *The Waste Land*:

> These fragments I have shored against my ruins.

And earlier in the same poem he speaks of

> A heap of broken images.

Eliot and Pound, in their very different ways, have always been learned men, deeply conscious of how much we owe to the past, and not only to our own Western past (from Greece and Rome, through Italy and France) but to the East, to Indian and Chinese cultures with entirely different concepts and modes from ours. The revolutionary poetry of Eliot and Pound is a learned, sometimes even a bookish, poetry; very different from the purely anarchic and deliberately iconoclastic work of the DADAists who were active on the Continent at about the same time; different, too, from the self-consciously modern poetry of such a man as the Italian, Marinetti, who believed that the past—even physically—should be destroyed: an idea which gave odd comfort to Mussolini's Fascists.

The ironical contrast which is the basis of such a poem as *The Waste Land* comes partly from this double view, of the present and the past. In times of great change, stress and uncertainty, the past seems particularly golden; this is reflected in the literature of the first half of the seventeenth century, under the shadow of the Civil War, and even more so in that of the twentieth century. Yet the present must be faced, and comfortable symbols from the literature of the past—the daffodil, the nightingale—cannot be used simply as talismans to ward off unpleasantness. This does not mean that a poet should deliberately load his poems with references to factory chimneys, turbines, slums, internal combustion engines and hydrogen bombs. These things are apt to be found in some sort of romantic, concealing dress; or a new and unsatisfactory myth is grafted on to the real facts. Stephen Spender's 'The Express' is an example of the first, the American poet Vachel Lindsay's 'The Kallyope Yell' of the second. Spender's is a piece of decoration, Lindsay's a deliberately crude attempt to identify itself with an aspect of the modern world. Spender romanticises, Lindsay simplifies; and so neither really succeeds. Or, to take another example, consider 'The Shadow of Cain' by Edith Sitwell; a poem which is ostensibly 'about' the dropping of the atomic bombs on Hiroshima and Nagasaki, but which is so crowded with portentous symbolism that the sheer horror of those events is hidden.

Eliot, as I show in a later chapter, established his link with tradition through his religion, and the symbolism in 'Ash Wednesday' and the *Four Quartets* is basically religious. But that was a later development, after *The Waste Land*, and the generation of the late nineteen twenties and early thirties (represented in my chapters on Auden, Spender, MacNeice and Day Lewis) tried to express what they felt to be a social sickness in social terms; hence Auden's 'smokeless chimneys, damaged bridges', Spender's picture of out-of-work men at street-corners, and the sometimes self-consciously contemporary imagery of MacNeice's and Day Lewis's verse of the 1930s. It is perhaps fashionable nowadays to be rather scornful of much of this work, superficial and crudely propagandist as some of it was; but at least these poets made a fair attempt to deal adequately and honestly with the modern world. And here, as elsewhere in literature, it is no good using the glib ready-made labels which have stuck through repetition.

The poets of the 1930s wrote much that was not overtly political—love poems, ballads, light verse, poems of personal problems; just as the term 'Angry Young Man' looks pretty silly and irrelevant when applied to such a poet of the 1950s as Philip Larkin, who writes a personal, sober, and unposturing poetry.

The charge of 'ugliness' which is commonly levelled at contemporary poetry is, I suppose, partly founded on the use of such specifically modern imagery as I have mentioned; but more, I think, on the break-up of traditional forms and whatever one means by 'poetic diction'. The language of the scene in the London pub in the second section of *The Waste Land* is, in isolation, certainly not poetry; one has to recognise that if one overheard such a conversation, in a pub or anywhere else, one would not regard it as having anything to do with a Wordsworth lyric or a Shakespeare sonnet. But there *is* poetry in Eliot's use of that language, and it lies in the juxtaposition—the placing side by side of the rich woman's boudoir and her neurosis on the one hand, and on the other the grim reality and the poverty-stricken language of the women in the pub; the emotional sterility of the rich and the attempt at physical sterility of the poor. I do not myself think that the pub passage is entirely successful (Eliot was really far too removed from the life and situation he was describing, I feel, to be entirely authentic and convincing); but conceptually, and to a fair extent actually, the piece is striking, and has poetic force and validity. Juxtaposition and contrast are part of the stuff of poetry; the Greek tragedians, in their use of irony, realised that thousands of years ago.

The fragmentation of modern life has its particular dangers for poetry, as for any other art; art, after all, is concerned with communication. W. B. Yeats, who struggled through much of his poetry with 'the fascination of what's difficult'—with

the attempt to shape, honestly and truthfully, recalcitrant
and awkward material—wrote in his *Autobiographies*:

> How small a fragment of our own nature can be brought to
> perfection, nor that even but with great toil, in a much divided
> civilization.

I said 'dangers', and by that meant that it is difficult (and
sometimes seems impossible) to make order out of chaos,
to make an experience or situation coherent and compre-
hensible to others. But that, of course, has always been the
job of art. The challenge does not preclude, but often stimu-
lates, the result. In one of his last poems, Yeats pondered the
genesis of his poetry, and realised that however obscure were
its beginnings (in the unconscious—'old kettles, old bottles
. . .'), the task of the poet is to deal honestly with whatever
he finds:

> Those masterful images because complete
> Grew in pure mind, but out of what began?
> A mound of refuse or the sweepings of a street,
> Old kettles, old bottles, and a broken can,
> Old iron, old bones, old rags, that raving slut
> Who keeps the till. Now that my ladder's gone,
> I must lie down where all the ladders start,
> In the foul rag-and-bone shop of the heart.

An act of communication presupposes an audience. And
the audience for poetry has unquestionably diminished since,
say, the time when a new book by Tennyson would be
eagerly awaited by a large public and would go into many
editions. It is, indeed, sometimes jokingly (or ruefully) said
that the only people today who read a new book of verse
by even a comparatively widely published poet are other
poets; and Dylan Thomas once characterised a mythical
little verse magazine as having a circulation of seventeen

poets and a woman who once met Kafka's aunt. This minimal audience in itself can be dangerous to poetry; it can encourage a clique or coterie approach, a reliance on private references and private jokes. The Victorian audience which supported Tennyson shared much of his background and ideas; it had, too, a natural—and cultivated—love of narrative and language; it was an audience which enjoyed three-volume novels, which saw verse as a good medium for telling a story, which listened to sermons with a critical ear for phrasing and rhetoric, and which liked word-games where verbal invention and a wide vocabulary counted for something. Without in any way starting on a tedious and false jeremiad about the evils of modern passive mass-entertainment, that is just not true today.

Alongside the shrinking of the audience for poetry has grown the shaping of literary criticism as a discipline, helped by the founding of departments of English literature in the universities at the end of the nineteenth century and beginning of the twentieth. Looking at it cynically, one can say that undergraduates who thought of reading English literature as a soft option were deliberately discouraged by dons who were keen to make the new faculty as 'respectable' (and stiff) as the old ones. It was not enough to read a poem; one had to dissect it, comment on it, demonstrate how it worked. And there is no great harm, and often may be great good, in that. No poem was ever killed through dissection. But *to the outsider*, the ordinary potential reader of poetry outside the university, the elaborate apparatus of literary criticism—or what appears to him to be that—encourages the always latent feeling that poetry is a mystery which only egg-heads can approach. And note that word 'approach', which is so common in literary discussion; it suggests a careful, and even circuitous, journey which must be undergone before one

gets even within shouting distance of the poem. So, as a
student audience for poetry has grown, a lay audience has
largely vanished.

It is easy, within the closed circle of a student audience, to
fall into a glib and slipshod critical jargon; to play what has
been called 'The Influence Game'—spending a great deal of
time pointing out what effect poets A, G, K and Z had, or
possibly had, on poet Y; or, most arid of all, and probably
commonest, especially in examinations, sticking to technique.
It is not enough to say, 'This is a sonnet, and therefore it
has 14 lines. The octave has such-and-such a rhyme-scheme,
and the sestet such-and-such. Alliteration is used in the fifth
and twelfth lines, and *shape* and *hope* in the sixth line are
internal half-rhymes,' and so on. That is not a study of
technique; it is a pseudo-mathematical exercise. Nor, at a
much less elementary but more pretentious and time-wasting
level, should one dally long with references to the 'dark
music' of the consonants and the 'thin whispers' of the
vowels. As F. R. Leavis has written:

> Questions of technique—versification, convention, relation
> of diction to the spoken language, and so on—cannot be isolated
> from considerations of fundamental purpose, essential ethos, and
> quality of life. That is, one can hardly say where technical
> questions turn into questions that one wouldn't ordinarily call
> technical.

In other words, a poem is in some sense a reflection of the life
it comes from; it cannot be disengaged from life, treated in
isolation as a piece of artistic mechanism. 'If poetry comes
not as naturally as the leaves to a tree', wrote Keats, 'it had
better not come at all.' And the reading of poetry should be
as natural as that, too—though that does not mean we should
not sometimes find ourselves puzzled by a poem, so that we

have to tease out the meaning by taking thought. The reader must sometimes be prepared to work almost as hard while he reads as the poet did while he wrote. Even the tree, in its instinctive way, puts a good deal of effort into making those leaves.

CHAPTER TWO

Gerard Manley Hopkins

(1844–1889)

When Robert Bridges in 1918 (twenty-nine years after Hopkins's death) brought out the first edition of *The Poems of Gerard Manley Hopkins*, he wrote a prefatory sonnet to the book, the last two lines of which address the poet in this way:

> Go forth: amidst our chaffinch flock display
> Thy plumage of far wonder and heavenward flight!

But this was prophecy rather than immediate fact; the 'chaffinch flock' of 1918 was not much better prepared for Hopkins than was the Victorian world in which he died— indeed, the poetic world of 1918 was *still* in many ways one determined by the precept and practice of the Victorians. It was not until a second edition appeared in 1930 (this time edited by Charles Williams) that Hopkins began to enjoy the reputation which has now raised him to the level of—in the eyes of many critics and readers—a major poet. In the words of Dr. F. R. Leavis (who did so much to introduce and establish Hopkins's work)

> He is likely to prove, for our time and the future, the only influential poet of the Victorian age, and he seems to me the greatest.

This forty-year neglect of Hopkins's poetry can be explained simply by referring to Bridges' introduction to the first edition, where Bridges seems to be a great deal on the defensive, acknowledging freely what he calls 'Oddity' and 'Obscurity', 'faults of taste' and 'blemishes in the poet's style'. Even the *Times Literary Supplement*, which in 1919 gave the book what must have seemed an astonishingly appreciative review, did not question these criticisms by Bridges; and though the review ends with the remark that the poems are 'authentic fragments that we trust even when they bewilder us', this is a fair example of its severe reservations:

> His worst trick is that of passing from one word to another . . . merely because they are alike in sound. This, at its worst, produces the effect almost of idiocy, of speech without sense and prolonged merely by echoes. It seems to be a bad habit, like stuttering, except that he did not strive against it.

The review does not quote any examples of this 'worst trick', but I imagine the critic was thinking of such a line as this, which Bridges condemns:

> as a stallion stalwart, very-violet-sweet.

But is this 'speech without sense and prolonged merely by echoes', is it an example (in Bridges' words) of 'affectation in metaphor'? Hopkins is here writing about the hills, which are the 'world-wielding' shoulder of God—massive, majestic, strong—and in the distance they have the same purple sheen as the muscular flank of a powerful horse; indeed, the hills rippling in the heat-haze seem to be powerfully muscled, as befits this anthropomorphic picture of the Creator of the earth. What better adjective *is* there than the powerful word 'stalwart', with all its implications of God's unshakeableness and imperturbability? The near-homophones 'stallion' and 'stalwart' slow up the movement deliberately, so that, as it were, the 'muscles' of the line flex slowly and powerfully. And, as a contrast, the compound adjective 'very-violet-sweet' moves rapidly and lightly; God and His creations are gentle as well as powerful. The movement is powerful, even frightening; the colour is delicate and gentle; and the combination is Hopkins's image of God.

An analysis of this sort is useful and necessary if one is not to be led into making charges such as those of Bridges and the *Times Literary Supplement*; but its danger is that it may distract one by emphasising too much *technical* considerations. Hopkins himself is perhaps partly to blame for this, because the Author's Preface which Bridges printed at the beginning of the first edition is wholly a guide, by Hopkins, to his own metrical rules. But one must think of this preface, not as an apologia or manifesto (such as Wordsworth's preface to the *Lyrical Ballads*) addressed to the public, but as a private synopsis of technical interest, from one practitioner to another. It is wrong to approach Hopkins's poetry by way of his own specialised nomenclature—Sprung Rhythm, Falling Feet, Outrides, Counterpoint Rhythm and so on. However, one certainly cannot, on the other hand, ignore the technique, and I shall return to it later.

The primary quality of Hopkins's poetry is energy. Energy was precisely what English poetry lacked during the Victorian period. To take two typical examples, Tennyson's 'Ulysses' and Browning's 'Saul'; Tennyson's poem is grave, thoughtful, elegiac, as (in a sense) befits the subject, but even in such meditative, slow-moving verse one ought to find some inner tension, some dynamic force behind the words. Instead, one feels that here is a mind moving in regular blank verse because it is easy for it to do so; technique has become habit. Browning's poem seems quite different; it appears to move vigorously, it is talking about physical action with what may appear to be physical excitement:

> Oh, the wild joys of living! the leaping from rock up to rock,
> The strong rending of boughs from the fir-tree, the cool
> > silver shock
> Of the plunge in a pool's living water, the hunt of the bear,
> And the sultriness showing the lion couched in his lair.

Yet two or three readings will begin to convince one that here, too, is a mind which has fallen into a set pattern because it requires no effort; the 'vigour' is revealed as merely a strong lurching beat—Tum-ti-tum-ti-ti-TUM-ti—ti-TUM-ti-ti-TUM-ti-ti-TUM. (I am not laughing at Browning; the brass-band noises represent what the first line really sounds like to me.)

Hopkins invented a name for this sort of thing. In a letter, written when he was only twenty, to an Oxford friend, he discussed what he called *Parnassian* poetry:

> It can only be spoken by poets, but is not in the highest sense poetry. It does not require the mood of mind in which the poetry of inspiration is written. It is spoken *on and from the level* of a poet's mind, not . . . when the inspiration, which is the gift of genius, raises him above himself.

And he goes on to say how most poets, great and minor, sooner or later develop their own brand of Parnassian, their own habitual way of saying things. A few moments thought will verify this. But to Hopkins, working in almost complete isolation, verse-writing was never a habit but a continually changing struggle with new material. His poetic energy itself came from two sources: first, from his close observation of, and excitement about, the natural world, in its most detailed and particularised forms; second, from the great stress caused not only by the violent, exultant effect of nature (amounting almost to hyperaesthesia), but also by the clash in his personality of the sensuous artist he naturally was and the ascetic Jesuit he had chosen to become. Very broadly, one can say that the first resulted in his excited, exuberant 'nature' poetry, emphasising the grandeur and glory of God; and the second in the dark, personal poems of spiritual combat. I shall deal with each in turn.

Nature (that is, all created things) was to Hopkins what the Sacraments are to all Christians: 'an outward and visible sign of an inward and spiritual grace'. Only man can see this sign and understand its meaning, can glorify God for the meaning behind the appearance and for the appearance itself:

> And what is Earth's eye, tongue, or heart else, where
> Else, but in dear and dogged man?

And nature reveals itself, not simply in one way, but in a variety which in every created object is different. This difference, this individual distinction, Hopkins called *inscape*; and the energy which determines that individuality, and which keeps it distinct, he called *instress*. He coined these two terms, just as he coined *Parnassian*, because a new concept demands a new word; and Hopkins's mind (controlled though it was by his self-imposed religious discipline) was startlingly original. Geoffrey Grigson has called Hopkins's poetry 'a passionate science'. It is a good phrase, for Hopkins observed and recorded with all the scrupulous exactness of a scientist, yet also with the passionate excitement of a poet. His Journals, written from 1866–75, show how minute and exact was his apprehension; everything, from the way a waterfall breaks up on the rocks below to the sensation of drawing one's hand through a cluster of damp bluebells, from the sequence of shapes into which a cloudbank breaks in the sky to the ooze which comes from the nostrils of a dying sheep, is caught and preserved. The observations, as they exist in the Journals, are perhaps closer to the scientist than to the poet; but they sparked into poetry. One year in particular—1877—was rich in poems which sprang from this observing and glorifying impulse; in that year he wrote 'God's Grandeur', 'The Starlight Night', 'Spring', 'The Sea and the Skylark', 'The Windhover', 'Pied Beauty' and 'Hurrahing in Harvest'. These, I feel, are the poems to which a reader unacquainted with Hopkins should first come, because they communicate most immediately the excitement, the individuality, the *instress* itself of his poetry. Hopkins himself described 'The Windhover' as 'the best thing I ever wrote'. It is a poem which has been much analysed and discussed by critics, not always helpfully; the best explication I know is given by Grigson in his 'Writers and their Work' pamphlet on Hopkins. But perhaps the poem which implicitly gives one the best 'feel' of Hopkins's excitement about instress and inscape is 'Pied Beauty'.

It is a poem of praise to God for the variousness of his creation; the beauty of the world, Hopkins says, is 'pied'— that is, variegated and parti-coloured, dappled and subtle. His method in the poem is to catalogue things which change from moment to moment, from season to season; things whose function, appearance, characteristics, mark them out separately and individually—the changing patterns of the sky, like the 'brinded' (brindled, dappled) hide of a cow; the small pink or red moles which lie, like stippled paint, on a trout's back; the contrast between the rich red-brown nut of the fallen chestnut and the green husk or case which encloses it, a contrast which he likens to the glowing flame which is revealed by breaking open a lit coal (this is very like the last two lines of 'The Windhover':

> . . . and blue-bleak embers, ah my dear,
> Fall, gall themselves, and gash gold-vermilion);

the varied browns and yellows of finches' wings; the patch-work of landscapes, changing, according to time and place, from the green of the fold where the animals are pastured to the dull fawn-brown of land left fallow and the rich deep brown of fields newly ploughed; all the specialist 'gear and tackle and trim' of man's different jobs—the fisherman's nets, floats and lines, the mechanic's spanner, wrench and grease-gun, and so on. Then, moving from particulars, he lists more generally the contrasts and antitheses of life which create instress and inscape—all things set in opposition, all things new or which strike one with a shock of newness, all things whose function is individual and economical ('spare'). All these things whose nature is 'freckled' with opposites in union are products of God, who 'fathers-forth' (analogous to 'bringing forth' a child). Yet God himself is 'past' (or 'above') change; he who creates is not the same as his creations; they are *signs* of his powers of invention, of individuation. These things 'praise him'; but the final words are really an imperative, addressed to man—'Praise him—it is your duty, and should be your delight, to do so.'

'Pied Beauty', as I have said, is a 'catalogue' poem; it is denotative in its method, indicating specific examples of God's variousness. A poem which puts Hopkins's ideas of 'selfhood' (essential individual quality) more generally and philosophically is 'As kingfishers catch fire, dragonflies draw flame', written four or five years after the six important 1877 poems. Everything, Hopkins says, has its own characteristics, through which it expresses its essential quality and the purpose for which it was made:

> Each mortal thing does one thing and the same:
> Deals out that being indoors each one dwells;
> Selves—goes itself; *myself* it speaks and spells,
> Crying *What I do is me: for that I came.*

But, more importantly—because man is God's highest creation on earth—man is the chief medium through whom God acts and reveals himself:

> I say more: the just man justices;
> Keeps grace: that keeps all his goings graces;
> Acts in God's eye what in God's eye he is—
> Christ—for Christ plays in ten thousand places,
> Lovely in limbs, and lovely in eyes not his
> To the Father through the features of men's faces.

Inadequate though man is, because God has chosen to act through him man himself must act through, and be witness of, all God's other creations: in some words from a sermon which Hopkins, as Jesuit priest, delivered—'Man was created to praise.'

This was Hopkins the passionate observer, excited by observation of nature in all its forms into an exultant poetic energy. But there was also the Hopkins who experienced agonising spiritual desolation, who bowed his will to the discipline of the order he had chosen, who struggled always to do his best as parish priest, as teacher, as man of God, yet who so often felt that he had failed. His clash of personality and will, aggravated by periodic bouts of ill-health, sometimes almost led him to despair, except that despair (which implies loss of faith in God's mercy) is treated by Roman Catholics as the deadliest of sins—and this itself must have set up tensions within him. The result is found in his so-called 'Terrible' sonnets of 1885—'Carrion Comfort', 'No worst, there is none', 'I wake and feel the fell of dark', 'Patience, hard thing!', 'My own heart let me more have pity on', and one or two others. There is energy here, too, but it is that of struggle, not exuberance.

Let us consider the poem 'I wake and feel the fell of dark'.

W. H. Gardner, one of the best Hopkins scholars, puts very well the basis of the poems of which this is one:

> Desolation is the human shuddering recoil from the strain of a rigorous discipline—a sourness, loss of hope, of joy, almost a suspension of faith itself, which makes the victim feel that he is totally separated from his God.

Yet, he continues,

> underneath the despair and complaint the note of willing self-surrender to the higher necessity is always implicit . . . (These poems) are the work of a man who, while putting the whole of his 'sad self' into a poem, could still preserve the sensitivity and control of the artist . . .

The poem begins with the impression of darkness and despair smothering light and hope; 'the fell of dark' should be taken in three senses—(1) the weight and smothering effect of an animal's 'fell' or hairy skin (2) the archaic adjective 'fell' used as a noun, to mean 'painfulness', 'ruthlessness', 'cruelty' (3) the dialect noun 'fell' (from the verb 'to fell'), meaning 'a knock-down blow'. The compound of these three senses is that he wakes and feels the heavy blow and cruel, crushing weight of night—with all its fears and night-mares—rather than the clear, kind light of day. His heart has been wandering through terrifying, uncharted darkness for the unimaginably long hours of the night, and is still condemned to it 'in yet longer light's delay'. He knows, through experience ('with witness'), that he has suffered and will continue to suffer this torture; in a great hyperbole of despair, he says that he is not speaking simply in terms of hours, of a short time, but of life. He calls constantly to God, but his cries are like letters sent to a distant country, letters which never arrive. God, indeed, seems to live very far away, and is so remote in the poet's despondency that he despairs of ever reaching him.

But the despair is, after all, part of the man himself; it is self-generated:

> I am gall, I am heartburn. God's most deep decree
> Bitter would have me taste: my taste was me;
> Bones built in me, flesh filled, blood brimmed the curse.

The 'selfyeast' of his spirit sours the 'dull dough' of his body; Hopkins takes his analogy from the making of bread, where the yeast acts by itself ('works', in the vocabulary of cooking) and makes the dough rise. It is, in other words, his selfish ego which makes his body, and hence his spirit, chafe and fret, souring his wholesomeness. Acknowledging this, he turns to consider 'the lost'—those in Hell—whose spiritual disease was close to his, and whose present state makes his own plight seem small: in paraphrase, 'I realise that those in Hell are in this condition, and that their torture—like mine—is that of being absolutely isolated in the Hell of their own selves (i.e. isolated, and thus cut off from God); but their torment— because it is absolute—is far worse than mine'. The final implication is that there is still hope; and that to be 'selved', 'inscaped' *absolutely* is the worst damnation. Thus the in- dividuation of the 'nature' poems is glorious because it is in relation to God; but individuation without such a relation is spiritual death.

Most readers of Hopkins will not be able fully to sym- pathise with the emotional conflict which forced these poems into being, because spiritual desolation is something from which they may feel remote; but there remains, in the finished product, 'the sensitivity and control of the artist'. He was a serious and dedicated craftsman, with an attitude to poetry which—despite his humility, his putting his job as a priest far above his 'secular' work—one must call professional. His journals and his letters to Bridges, R. W. Dixon and Coventry Patmore show that. And his technique, though it is based on much scholarly inquiry into Latin, Greek, Welsh and English (standard, archaic and dialect English) metrics and vocabulary, was not mere invention in the void; it was formed and perfected because only in these metres, in these words, could he best say what he had to say. Yeats made a great mistake when he called Hopkins's manner 'a last development of poetic diction', for poetic diction—language at several elegant removes from life—was precisely what Hopkins avoided. In a letter to Bridges, he wrote:

> Poetical language should be the current language heightened, to any degree heightened and unlike itself, but not . . . an obsolete one. This is Shakespeare's and Milton's practice.

But he added—and this is important—'passing freaks and graces are another thing'. Hopkins's poetry is written, as some critics have maintained all true poetry is written, in a language of excitement; it is thus very much 'heightened' language, and the 'passing freaks and graces' add to the individual quality of the excitement. Hopkins was one of the very few linguistic innovators in the English language, along with Shakespeare, Milton and Joyce; he used the full resources of the language and, when those resources seemed to be inadequate, he invented. By 'full resources', I mean his employment of specialist words (such as 'sillion' in 'The Windhover'), dialect words (such as 'degged' in 'Inversnaid' and 'fashed' in 'The Leaden Echo and the Golden Echo'), his rich use of alliteration, internal rhyme, assonance, dissonance; and he invented compound words with the energy of a man whose mind enjoyed all the cognate and sound-linked shades of language: 'spendsavour salt', 'beadbonny ash', 'selfyeast of spirit', 'wanwood', 'leafmeal'. Like Shakespeare, he forced language into his own mould, making words do service as new parts of speech—nouns become verbs, adjectives become adverbs; and unnecessary words—very often definite or indefinite articles and relative pronouns—are ruthlessly omitted.

As for his metrical technique, which I mentioned earlier in this chapter, perhaps only one thing needs to be said about Sprung Rhythm: that it reads, and scans, purely by stress and not by number of syllables. This means that language does not need to be forced on to a Procrustean bed of metre. Hopkins himself expressed it lucidly enough in a letter to Bridges:

> Why do I employ sprung rhythm at all? Because it is the nearest to the rhythm of prose, that is the native and natural rhythm of speech, the least forced, the most rhetorical and emphatic of all rhythms, combining, as it seems to me, opposite and, one would have thought, incompatible excellences, markedness of rhythm—that is rhythm's self—and naturalness of expression . . .

To get the full force of his rhythms, one should read 'The Wreck of the Deutschland' (the long poem with which he resumed his poetic career in 1875, after a self-imposed silence of seven years) and 'The Leaden Echo and the Golden Echo'; admittedly both these poems are initially difficult, but in reading them one should take Hopkins's advice: 'take breath and read it with the ears, as I always wish to be read, and my verse becomes all right.' Above all, the energy in Hopkins's poetry has a truly physical quality; it becomes the thing it is about. Reading it requires a pleasurable and bracing physical effort, and the 'way into' his work itself grows clearer.

Can poets learn from Hopkins? The answer to this must be qualified. Certainly they can learn the possibilities of language, the way in which rhetoric can be used in a different way from that of the Elizabethan dramatists, Donne, Milton and Yeats, and also the importance of sound; but one can almost make it a rule that he cannot be learned from *directly*— that is, he is in no ordinary sense a possible, or good, model. Dylan Thomas came closest to learning directly from him, while Hopkins's influence on Auden, Day Lewis and George Barker has been much more superficial and also much more dangerous. The uniqueness of his life, his vocation and his personality sets him apart as much as Joyce when Joyce wrote *Finnegan's Wake*. But it is not the chief importance of writers to be influences or influenced; and there are some whose very isolation makes them the more extraordinary.

CHAPTER THREE

W. B. Yeats

(1865–1939)

Shortly before his death in 1939, Yeats asked the Cambridge critic T. R. Henn what he valued most in his poetry: Henn answered 'Wisdom'. This is not an obvious answer, but it has a good deal of truth in it. 'Wisdom', like 'virtue', is almost an old-fashioned word in English today; 'intelligent' is a more frequent epithet of praise than 'wise', and 'wisdom', perhaps we tend to think, is for the old and serene; for those who sit and vegetate rather than for those who move and feel. Yet Yeats was certainly one who moved actively and felt passionately, never more so than in the later years of his life. He wrote in 'The Spur':

> You think it horrible that lust and rage
> Should dance attention upon my old age;
> They were not such a plague when I was young;
> What else have I to spur me into song?

Yeats's wisdom was that of a man who had built slowly and painfully on a lifetime of experience. Until the age of about 40, he was little more than a talented minor poet, with five books published, and a reputation which linked him— personally and stylistically—with the 'decadent' poets, Lionel Johnson, Arthur Symons, Ernest Dowson. G. S. Fraser, in his British Council pamphlet on Yeats, convincingly quotes statements by various critics who at different times were 'convinced that Yeats was finished'. Looking back now and seeing his work in perspective, we can see that there is a perceptible change which begins with the publication of his volume *The Green Helmet* in 1910, becomes more obvious in *Responsibilities* (1914), and turns into a wholly individual voice in *Michael Robartes and the Dancer* (1921). The last twenty years of his life (1919–1939) produced his finest poetry—a culmination unique in the history of English literature—yet if we characterise wisdom as being a primary quality in his best work, we must not assume that it is the calm wisdom of a contented old man. Rather, Yeats implicitly understood Blake's maxim that 'The road of excess leads to the palace of wisdom.'

But by 'the road of excess' I do not mean something akin to Rimbaud's insistence on 'the derangement of all the senses'. Outwardly, Yeats's life as a man was not eventful in any Bohemian way, despite the company he kept in his youth. He proceeded through a long, frustrating love-affair with one woman to a happy marriage with another; a combination of circumstances and his own will forced him to become, for many years, a man of affairs; and both provided him with much nourishment for his poetry. Yet the sexual lust and the political rage which sprang from these were always controlled by a firmness and discipline which were often at their best when struggling to tame recalcitrant material. He knew, in his own words, 'the fascination of what's difficult'.

Yeats's own peculiar distillation of wisdom can be said to come from two main sources: his sense of nobility and his sense of reverence. Speaking of his own Irish generation of poets—Synge, Gogarty, George Russell—he wrote (in 'Coole Park and Ballylee'):

> We were the last romantics—chose for theme
> Traditional sanctity and loveliness;
> Whatever's written in what poets name
> The book of the people; whatever most can bless
> The mind of man or elevate a rhyme.

'Traditional sanctity and loveliness' was something Yeats valued deeply, and it is this 'traditionalism' which sometimes inspires accusations that Yeats was reactionary, even fascist. Certainly he was no egalitarian; one remembers his rather unpleasant sneer, 'base-born products of base beds'. But his lament for an order that was passing was not merely for the great houses and the aristocracy which lived in them; it was a lament for man's rootlessness and lack of coherence. Again and again this contrast between rootlessness and a sense of place, between elegance and formlessness, is treated in Yeats's work. He saw people in the great city masses as restless, nomadic, and we read elsewhere in 'Coole Park and Ballylee':

> Where fashion or mere fantasy decrees
> We shift about—all that great glory spent—
> Like some poor Arab tribesman and his tent.

A good poem in which to find set down those human qualities which Yeats valued most highly is 'A Prayer for my Daughter'; he wishes her beauty (though his qualification of this is important, and I shall return to it later); courtesy; roots in 'one dear perpetual place'; lack of hatred; self-reliance; and—most important of all—a life based on 'ceremony' and 'custom', two words which are really pivots on which the whole poem turns. They can be considered to be other aspects of what above I called 'nobility' and 'reverence'.

> Ceremony's a name for the rich horn,
> And custom for the spreading laurel tree.

By 'the rich horn' Yeats means the Horn of Plenty, the cornucopia, the gifts with which a fortunate child is born; a birthright he has already referred to in the fourth and eighth stanzas of the poem. In particular, he means by 'ceremony' the gift of living one's life with a cool elegance, as a ritual. As for the laurel, it is introduced in the sixth stanza as a symbol of rootedness; he prays that his daughter may

> live like some green laurel
> Rooted in one dear perpetual place.

In other words, may the child have that sense of belonging which comes to people who have lived long and happily in one place, identifying themselves with that place: it is an implicit protest against the rootlessness of modern urban civilisation

Yeats himself was literally rootless and restless for much of his life, but he found emotional nourishment in his ancestral Ireland. From his early days, he was steeped in Irish mythology and folk-lore, but in the poems of his youth the tales and legends were fanciful rather than truly imaginative (to make Coleridge's distinction). Towards the end of his life, he dismissed them contemptuously as

> Themes . . . that might adorn old songs or courtly shows.

Even when his themes were not of Cathleen ni Houlihan, wandering Aengus, Oisin and other misty figures of the Celtic past, the world of his early poems was one of personal daydreams. One of his most famous poems, 'The Lake Isle of Innisfree' (from *The Rose*, 1893), probably owes its popular success to the fact that it gives substance to a daydream that many people have—of withdrawing from the bustle and worry of the world to a country retreat. Yet this retreat is—in the manner of daydreams—only vaguely described, despite the seeming particularity of the 'nine bean-rows' and the 'hive for the honey-bee'. It is, in fact, a sentimental poem, if we take sentimentality to be 'feeling in excess of the situation presented'. The Ireland of 'The Lake Isle' is something Yeats consciously rejected in later years; in his poem

'The Municipal Gallery Revisited' (from *Last Poems*, 1939)
he accepted the new Ireland.

> This is not
> The dead Ireland of my youth, but an Ireland
> The poets have imagined, terrible and gay.

The change in his attitude was brought about by the
changing situation in Ireland itself. During the First World
War, while Britain was preoccupied with the war against
the Central Powers, southern Ireland rebelled, and later pro-
claimed itself a republic; fierce fighting broke out in 1916,
and continued sporadically until 1921, with northern and
southern Ireland virtually involved in civil war, and with
much brutality on the part of both the Irish and the British.
The history of the Irish people, with its repression from
Cromwell onwards, the hunger for land and for food, the
fanaticism of battling factions and ideologies, determined
how bitter would be the struggle. As Yeats put it in his
poem 'Remorse for Intemperate Speech' (1931):

> Out of Ireland have we come.
> Great hatred, little room,
> Maimed us at the start.
> I carry from my mother's womb
> A fanatic heart.

Yeats was ambivalent in his attitude towards this hatred and
violence; it was part of a struggle for the independence of
his native country, at times it seemed glorified as something
through which men struggled towards greatness and nobility,
yet also it was something which soured and destroyed men;
and the violence then was not an expression of patriotism
but merely that of 'weasels fighting in a hole'. Elsewhere,
he was stricken with remorse because he thought that he

himself, as a known supporter of Irish nationalism, might
have been partly responsible for the hatred and bloodshed:

> Come fix upon me that accusing eye,
> I thirst for accusation. All that was said,
> All that was sung in Ireland is a lie
> Bred out of the contagion of the throng.

Or, more starkly, his direct questioning of guilt:

> Did that play of mine send out
> Certain men the English shot . . . ?
> Could my spoken words have checked
> That whereby a house lay wrecked?

Yeats's desire for Ireland's independence was a product of
emotion rather than politics; and, as an Irishman passionately
attached to his country by ties of ancestry and pride in his
country's history and legends, he gradually became disillusioned because he felt that at the heart of the violence and
hatred by the Irish political leaders and journalists was a
meanness of spirit, a selfishness and lack of breeding which
was poisoning the heroic Irish nobility. Writing of this
decay, he found his symbol of the old heroism in O'Leary,
the Irish leader who struggled with Gladstone for Irish
Home Rule and who died in 1907 before seeing to what
depths that struggle for independence had come:

> What need you, being come to sense,
> But fumble in a greasy till
> And add the halfpence to the pence
> And prayer to shivering prayer until
> You have dried the marrow from the bone;
> For men were born to pray and save:
> Romantic Ireland's dead and gone;
> It's with O'Leary in the grave.

Yeats felt he wanted little to do with an Ireland whose spirit had become coarsened. Three events in particular, even before the beginning of the 1916 fighting, convinced him of this coarsening: the first was the desecration of Parnell, Ireland's greatest nationalist leader, who, at the very height of his popularity and political power, had been discovered to be having an adulterous affair with a married woman. As soon as this scandal was revealed, Parnell was reviled by the mob and driven into exile. Yeats believed in Parnell's greatness, and was disgusted by the hypocritical outcry of the Dublin newspapers and the Dublin people, who with such fickleness could abandon a man whom a moment before they had seemed to idolise. The second event was the rejection of Sir Hugh Lane's magnificent collection of pictures by the Dublin Corporation—on the grounds that the city rates would have to be raised in order to buy a site and build an art gallery. This convinced Yeats of the new philistinism of Ireland. The third event (and the one closest to Yeats's heart) was the violent reception given to Synge's play *The Playboy of the Western World*. Synge was a friend of Yeats from early days; they had shared lodgings when Synge was in his early twenties, and Yeats, being rather older, had encouraged Synge in his writing, especially in his interest in Irish dialect and folk-lore and their suitability to drama. *The Playboy of the Western World* drew on the Irish peasantry whose speech and traditions meant so much to Yeats—their racy talk, their mythology, and their simple physical violence; their emotional gullibility and their delight in audaciousness for its own sake. Yet when Synge's play was performed, it was taken by the Irish nationalist press to be a slur on Ireland; the journalists saw—or pretended to see—Irishmen being presented as rustic fools, as ignorant simpletons and stage comics. The play was booed off the stage; the actors were

bombarded with letters asking why they allowed themselves
to be associated with such 'decadent filth'. Everywhere the
philistines seemed to have triumphed. Yeats saw in 'the
leaders of the crowd' who had achieved this that

> They must to keep their certainty accuse
> All that are different of a base intent;
> Pull down established honour; hawk for news
> Whatever their loose fantasy invent
> And murmur it with bated breath . . .

Popularity seemed to imply crudeness, hatred, lies, all that
'baseness' which Yeats found most distasteful.

Yeats's link with Irish nationalism was not simply one of
disillusioned patriotic sentiment, however; it was also one of
love, in the person of Maud Gonne, the most important
woman in his life until his marriage (and even, perhaps,
after that). Maud Gonne was a famous beauty, and also a
woman of great intellect and passion, with whom Yeats had
fallen in love at their first meeting in 1889. Yet his love was
a hopeless one. For years they were associated together in
Yeats's work for the theatre, in nationalist political and
literary meetings all over Ireland, in their sharing of Yeats's
own work in poetry; yet she always refused to marry him
and, quite suddenly in 1903, married instead one of the Irish
nationalist leaders, John MacBride. Yeats saw this beautiful
woman become a political demagogue, an arouser of political
hatred. Yet he blamed neither her nor MacBride for this
gradual change; he blamed himself, his timidity, his naive
concern with political 'affairs' which he did not understand.
As Richard Ellmann says, 'Yeats, until his thirty-seventh
year, had remained in his love affair a wide-eyed boy'. He
had exalted Maud Gonne to the position of his Muse; he had
leaned too heavily on her, and on his dreams generally, and
now he had to learn to face reality.

What he learned to do in his poetry, in fact, was to base himself on the harsh substance of life. This is the theme of one of his last poems, 'The Circus Animals' Desertion'—the abandonment of 'allegorical dreams' and the realisation that

> I must lie down where all the ladders start,
> In the foul rag-and-bone shop of the heart.

And his disillusion over his affair with Maud Gonne brought him to see that what the human spirit needs above all is balance—analogous to 'the need for roots' in a place and a way of life. Beauty and violence, which before he had tended to romanticise, he now saw to be potentially dangerous. In 'Prayer for my Daughter', he considers Helen and Aphrodite ('that great Queen, that rose out of the spray'), and maintains that it was their perfect beauty that led them astray:

> It's certain that fine women eat
> A crazy salad with their meat
> Whereby the Horn of Plenty is undone.

As for violence, which stems from hatred, 'an intellectual hatred is the worst'; Maud Gonne, beautiful and brilliant, tarnished that beauty with the ferocity of her mind's hatred—hatred which was a product of that very brilliance:

> Have I not seen the loveliest woman born
> Out of the mouth of Plenty's horn,
> Because of her opinionated mind
> Barter that horn and every good
> By quiet natures understood
> For an old bellows full of angry wind?

Yeats's realisation of tradition as the thing that gives us balance made him aware of history and myth in a new way; not as

> Themes . . . that might adorn old songs or courtly shows

but as patterns of behaviour and action which control man's life; what has happened will happen again; the gyre or circle of history is continually turning, dragging in its wake a succession of consequences. Yeats's attitude to history often seems fanciful and wilfully obscure, if one takes too seriously his quasi-scientific approach. But his large prose book on the subject, *A Vision*, should be considered as a poetic source-book rather than as a scientific work—though I think Kenneth Allott is making a wrong emphasis when he calls it 'of importance for the poet's idea of magic'. Yeats was interested in, and to some extent convinced by, magic; but history to him was not controlled by magic but by a pattern of destiny —not the same thing at all.

This pattern of destiny or succession of consequences is the theme of his strange, powerful sonnet 'Leda and the Swan'. It is Yeats's version of the words Eliot gives to Becket in *Murder in the Cathedral*:

> I know that history at all time draws
> The strangest consequence from remotest cause.

Leda, a beautiful Queen of Sparta, was (according to legend) noticed by Zeus, the greatest of the gods on Olympus, who descended to earth in the form of a swan and raped her. Leda consequently gave birth to two eggs, from one of which Helen was born—Helen, whose seduction by Paris was the cause of the Trojan War, which in its turn caused the birth of the Greek nation, which in its turn laid the foundations of modern Europe . . . and so on. The poem first gives us a violent sensual picture of the rape itself, the clash between animal and human, God and man. Implicit in the picture, in the act itself, is the realisation that from it will result Love and War, the two activities which Helen symbolises; so that the birth of western civilisation is also the birth of two of man's primary passions, lust and violence. Zeus, as the supreme god, must have realised these consequences, but did Leda, the passive woman through whom history enacted itself?

> Did she put on his knowledge with his power
> Before the indifferent beak could let her drop?

And this clash of human and divine is also suggestive of a greater Annunciation—that of Mary the mother of Christ:

> When that fierce virgin and her Star
> Out of the fabulous darkness called.

Yeats was not a Christian; yet he felt that there were certain moments in history when the human came into contact with the divine, the divine 'accomplished his predestined will', and thenceforth the order of things was changed. The human and the divine take many forms, but there is continuity in both. It is significant that, when Yeats edited the *Oxford Book of Modern Verse*, he chose as the first passage in the book a piece which is not a poem at all but which moved him with the power of poetry: Pater's passage about the 'Mona Lisa', taken from his essay on Leonardo da Vinci and printed as free verse. Pater saw her as a mysterious eternal figure, re-appearing in history in different forms, but somehow always the same. 'Everything changes, everything is the same': such was Yeats's view of history.

Yet perhaps Yeats's most enduring poetry stems neither from his attitude to politics or history, nor from his unhappy love for Maud Gonne, but from the unquenchable and continually unsatisfied *generalised* passion of his old age:

> I have not lost desire
> But the heart that I had;
> I thought 'twould burn my body
> Laid on the death-bed,
> For who could have foretold
> That the heart grows old?

The cry was not always that of an old man whose desire had outstripped his body; Yeats had moved through the years to a stark, impersonal strength—the *impersonal* strength which is characteristic of almost all great poetry. Looked at in this way, the poems in *Words for Music Perhaps*, *A Woman Young and Old* and *Last Poems* can be seen as the crowning success in Yeats's search for a *persona*, or mask: the projection of a situation and a voice into other people—Crazy Jane, for instance, or the Lady and the Chambermaid. There is no trace here of the loose, vague, delicate, insubstantial and essentially self-pitying romanticism of the early Yeats; there is no wastage of sentiment or of words. He objectified his own desires, and set them in the body and spirit and words of a woman, as in 'The Lady's First Song':

> I turn round
> Like a dumb beast in a show,
> Neither know what I am
> Nor where I go,
> My language beaten
> Into one name;
> I am in love
> And that is my shame.
> What hurts the soul
> My soul adores,
> No better than a beast
> Upon all fours.

Sidney Keyes, the young poet who was killed in the Second World War, pointed out that in the correspondence between Yeats and Dorothy Wellesley (whom Yeats got to know late in life), Yeats always seemed to write as the woman and Dorothy Wellesley as the man. Yeats indeed in his old age took upon himself a sort of androgynous, Tiresias-like quality, an ability to sound the depths of both man and woman; and the depths were physical, not intellectual. At his most extreme, he seems to reject any view of man which does not see him as a simple, desiring animal. Taking some words by Thomas Mann as his preface—'In our time the destiny of man presents itself in political terms'—he wrote his poem, 'Politics', which shows how alien to Yeats was Mann's attitude. The scene is a party, full of distinguished and brilliant men—politicians, journalists, men of affairs—discussing the world situation. Yeats sees near him a young and beautiful girl, and her presence distracts him from the abstract talk, so that he cannot fix his attention

> On Roman or on Russian
> Or on Spanish politics.
> Yet here's a travelled man that knows
> What he talks about,
> And there's a politician
> That has read and thought,
> And maybe what they say is true
> Of war and war's alarms
> But O that I were young again
> And held her in my arms!

Such an attitude can be called irresponsible, and if it were the only attitude in Yeats's later work one would—perhaps reluctantly—have to reject Henn's answer, 'Wisdom'. Yet there is a toughness of spirit, an integrity of purpose, about these last poems which compel one to admire and believe them. In the words of Auden's elegy for Yeats,

> You were silly like us; your gift survived it all.

Yeats's 'silliness' was lack of what the world calls common-sense; but common-sense and wisdom are not the same thing. Yeats's philosophy—insofar as it revealed itself in his prose and in his personal life—was a hotch-potch, in many ways, of stoicism, mysticism and nonsense, culled from omnivorous reading and his own frustrations and doubts (experienced in the Irish troubles, in his love-affairs, and in his own struggle to face the harsh reality I have spoken of). Yet out of all this rag-bag of half-digested and spurious knowledge, of human mistakes and vanities, came the greatest, and some of the wisest, poetry of this century. His 'Prayer for Old Age' both states his own dilemma and acts as his own arrogant—and humble—epitaph:

> God guard me from those thoughts men think
> In the mind alone;
> He that sings a lasting song
> Thinks in a marrow-bone;
>
> From all that makes a wise old man
> That can be praised of all;
> O what am I that I should not seem
> For the song's sake a fool?
>
> I pray—for fashions' word is out
> And prayer comes round again—
> That I may seem, though I die old,
> A foolish, passionate man.

CHAPTER FOUR

Wilfred Owen

(1893–1918)

D. H. Lawrence

(1885–1930)

When the First World War began in 1914, the poet who most quickly seemed to catch the mood of the moment was Rupert Brooke. Even before his death in 1915, he had become almost a legend: the young, handsome Renaissance man whose poetry, it seemed to many people at that time, had an Elizabethan vigour. Two of his sonnets from the short sequence called *1914* are probably still among the best-known poems among English people, known by millions of people whom poetry does not otherwise touch: 'Peace' and 'The Soldier'.

Yet Brooke's poetry is unsatisfactory; it aims at profundity, but never manages to catch more than a superficial romanticism, an adolescent concern with words which—in the context of his poems—are simply vague emotional counters: *Beauty, Love, April, bright, fragrance, tenderness, Death.* Dr. Leavis, in a few typically acidulous but also just words, has characterised him thus: 'He energised the Garden Suburb ethos with a certain original talent and the vigour of a prolonged adolescence'.

Brooke's attitude to the war was naturally romantic; it would be odd for it to have been otherwise at that time. But soon—certainly by 1916—it was no longer possible to think of war 'as swimmers into cleanness leaping'; the trench warfare and the battles dragged on, and poets such as Siegfried Sassoon and Edmund Blunden began to express in their poetry more realistically and satirically the waste and horror of war. It is Wilfred Owen, however, who has come to be seen as the finest poet of the war period, though it took some time after his death in 1918 and the publication of his *Poems* in 1920 for his importance to be widely recognised. Up until about 1916, he was a fairly conventional poet, imitative of Keats and Tennyson. He had spent a year or so in France just before the war, teaching and studying, and it is there that he began to use his characteristic half-rhymes, perhaps in imitation of French poetry; at first quite deliberately, in the nature of an ingenious technical exercise:

> Leaves
> 　　Murmuring by myriads in the shimmering trees.
> Lives
> 　　Wakening with wonder in the Pyrenees.
> Birds
> 　　Cheerily chirping in the early day.
> Bards
> 　　Singing of summer scything thro' the hay . . .

But later the device came to be more than simply a device: as Edmund Blunden has written 'again and again by means of it he creates remoteness, darkness, emptiness, shock, echo, the last word'. These effects, having their origins in his grim and disordered life as an infantry officer in France, made his poetry individual in a way that it was not before; it matured extraordinarily quickly, in the urgent atmosphere which war brings. A little over a year before his death, he wrote in a letter:

> Tennyson, it seems, was always a great child. So should I have been, but for Beaumont Hamel [a part of the front line in

France where there was particularly heavy fighting]. Not before January 1917 did I write the *only* lines of mine that carry the stamp of maturity.

The lines he refers to are from 'Happiness', written shortly before 'Exposure', one of his best poems. In the brief two years or less during which he wrote all the poems by which he is best-known, he grew, not in sensitiveness—that was there already, in the Keats-and-Tennyson poems—but in depth; his innate romantic and sensuous temperament was disciplined and made more powerful by coming to terms with a harsher reality:

Our brains ache, in the merciless iced east winds that knive us . . .
Wearied we keep awake because the night is silent . . .
Low, drooping flares confuse our memory of the salient . . .
Worried by silence, sentries whisper, curious, nervous,
    But nothing happens.

Yet the romanticism was still there; and it was this which Yeats was really criticising when he refused to include any of Owen's poems in the *Oxford Book of Modern Verse*. 'Passive suffering,' wrote Yeats, 'is not a theme for poetry'; but he refers elsewhere (in one of his letters to Dorothy Wellesley) to Owen's poetry as 'all blood and sucked sugar-stick'. In other words, Yeats's idea of the hero could not comprehend, and certainly could not sympathise with, a romanticism so different from his own; to Yeats, Owen's compassion seemed mere self-pity and morbid self-indulgence. But there is much more relevance and truth than Yeats's opinions allow in Owen's own preface to the poems, written when he was thinking of gathering them together for a book:

This book is not about heroes. English Poetry is not yet fit to speak of them.

Nor is it about deeds, or lands, or anything about glory,
honour, might, majesty, dominion, or power, except War.
Above all, I am not concerned with Poetry.
My subject is War, and the pity of War.
The Poetry is in the pity.
Yet these elegies are to this generation in no sense consolatory.
They may be to the next. All a poet can do to-day is warn.
That is why the true Poets must be truthful.

'Above all, I am not concerned with Poetry'; by this he
means attitudinising about war, romance putting the gilt on
reality:

> But they are troops who fade, not flowers
> For poets' tearful fooling.

The poet's job is not to embroider but to warn. Thus the
monitory, didactic, moralising element is strong in Owen's
poems. They taste of their period, too, and in few cases could
they have been written under the circumstances of the
Second World War; they are products of the wastefulness,
dirt, muddle and boredom of trench warfare, as well as
of the more active aspects of the war. The action that *is*
there tends to be brutish and unheroic, as in 'Mental
Cases', 'S.I.W.', 'The Dead Beat', 'À Terre' and, more
impersonal and less fiercely and savagely indignant, 'Strange
Meeting'.

There are others, such as 'Inspection', which are quite as
colloquial, satirical and sharp as anything Sassoon ever wrote,
and there may indeed be some influence here, for Owen and
Sassoon saw a good deal of one another during one stage of
the war, when they were in the same officers' hospital.
Something of what he felt for Sassoon, and something of the
individuality of Owen's letters, can be seen in the following

excerpt from a letter to his fellow-patient, written after he had left hospital:

> Know that since mid-September, when you still regarded me as a tiresome little knocker on your door, I held you as Keats + Christ + Elijah + my colonel + my father-confessor + Amenophis IV in profile. What's that mathematically?

But Owen's poetry, despite its basic romanticism, is of a quite different kind from Sassoon's; his sense of form was more adventurous, more genuinely empirical, than that of any other young poet of the period, and in his best work the urgency of what he is saying forces out images and lines which seem to dictate their own form. Look, for instance, at 'Insensibility', where the loose line structure and the variable stresses echo the mingled doubt and definitiveness of what is being said:

> Happy are men who yet before they are killed
> Can let their veins run cold.
> Whom no compassion fleers
> Or makes their feet
> Sore on the alleys cobbled with their brothers.
> The front line withers,
> But they are troops who fade, not flowers
> For poets' tearful fooling:
> Men, gaps for filling:
> Losses who might have fought
> Longer; but no one bothers.

And later:

> Having seen all things red,
> Their eyes are rid
> Of the hurt of the colour of blood for ever.

Here the two short lines with their monosyllabic half-rhymes, stab home quickly before the long line, whose disillusionment and weariness is stressed by that very length and by the repeated 'of . . . of . . .of', throwing the stress on to 'hurt . . . colour . . . blood' and dying away in the unstressed 'for ever'.

'If Owen had lived . . . ?' The question is a fairly idle but natural one. People have asked it about Keats for long enough. I cannot feel that he would have relaxed into a gentle and occasional poet as, in their different ways, Sassoon and Blunden have done. Nor do I feel that he had the sort of quirky individuality which has helped to make Graves the adaptable and inventive poet he has become. Perhaps he would simply have stopped writing, once the war was over. Whatever the answer to the unanswerable, Owen's poetry remains as both an important fragment of historical importance—an atmospheric picture of a particularly unpleasant and futile war—and as a body of work satisfying in itself, and also full of unquarried poetic raw material. It is true that Auden and Day Lewis, to name only two, have put to some advantage specific technical devices which they learned directly from Owen's poetry; but I hope I have shown that more than mere technical devices can, with sensitiveness, be learned from it.

D. H. LAWRENCE

D. H. Lawrence was not, of course, primarily a poet; his main reputation rests on his novels, which in some cases have been claimed to be the major literary works of the century. Yet he began as a poet, and the temper and atmosphere of his novels is very often poetic. Edmund Wilson, the American critic, has written:

> Would not D. H. Lawrence . . . if he had lived a century earlier, probably have told his tales, as Byron and Crabbe did: in verse? Is it not just as correct to consider him the last of the great English romantic poets as one of the most original of modern English novelists?

But, making a formal distinction between the techniques of poetry and prose, Lawrence was not a great poet. His sensibility, his intensity, his impressionistic and symbolical gifts (for example, the scene in *Women in Love* where Birkin throws stones into the moon's reflection in a pool), his dithyrambic rhythms and his repetitions—all these, in his novels, are *close* to poetry, or are part of the raw material of poetry; but Lawrence, when writing poetry as such, seldom paid enough attention to received poetic forms to shape his ideas into more than notes towards poems. Indeed, he despised what I call received poetic forms: 'Remember, skilled verse is dead in fifty years.' What he aimed at, he said, was 'a free, essential verse, that cuts to the centre of things.' But it is oddly difficult to escape from form in poetry, even if one wants to, for words fall naturally into patterns (they certainly did in Lawrence's prose), and the patterns that Lawrence tended to adopt in his poems were those of Whitman, and, ultimately, the Authorised Version of the Bible; a form as unnatural as that of the sonnet, though far more difficult to handle well.

Lawrence's best poems are those which keep their eyes solidly on the object, describing and evoking without too much of a didactic or moralising burden. Several of the poems from *Birds, Beasts and Flowers* come into this category:

'Snake', 'Kangaroo', 'The Mosquito', 'Bat'. The moralising
element is there in all of them, but there is also enough
natural perception (the way a snake drinks, the way a kangaroo
hops, the way a mosquito approaches its victim, the way a
bat swoops) to make a firm basis, a sort of logical jumping-
off place, for the moral. In 'Snake', for example:

> He lifted his head from drinking, as cattle do,
> And looked at me vaguely, as drinking cattle do,
> And flickered his two-forked tongue from his lips, and mused a
>   moment,
> And stooped and drank a little more,
> Being earth-brown, earth-golden from the burning bowels of the
>   earth
>
> On the day of Sicilian July, with Etna smoking.

That is accurately and beautifully said; and it gives us the
sort of 'evidence' we need to experience and sympathise
with the conclusion—that, after frightening away the snake,

>   . . . immediately I regretted it.
> I thought how paltry, how vulgar, what a mean act!
> I despised myself and the voices of my accursed human education . . .
> And so, I missed my chance with one of the lords
> Of life.
> And I have something to expiate;
> A pettiness.

In his less successful poems, there is too much unsupported
statement, too much badgering of the reader and hammering
of the insistent point; the tone of voice becomes harsh,
strained and, in the end, nagging; the reader feels that he is
being 'got at'—which is perhaps what Lawrence wanted,

but not at the expense of losing the reader. This sort of thing:

> I wish people, when you sit near them,
> wouldn't think it necessary to make conversation
> and send thin draughts of words
> blowing down your neck and your ears
> and giving you a cold in your inside.

That makes its point—but in what a lame, querulous, unpointed way. It is poor verse and poor satire.

But there are other poems, most of them among his early work, which are concerned with making a more formal statement, and yet which keep a vividness and freshness that come from personal observation. Such poems are 'Piano' and 'Discord in Childhood'; and 'Giorno Dei Morti', written during his first stay in Italy, in 1912–13, and describing an Italian country funeral:

> Along the avenue of cypresses,
> All in their scarlet cloaks and surplices
> Of linen, go the chanting choristers,
> The priests in gold and black, the villagers . . .
>
> And all along the path to the cemetery
> The round dark heads of men crowd silently
> And black-scarved faces of womenfolk, wistfully
> Watch at the banner of death, and the mystery.
>
> And at the foot of a grave a father stands
> With sunken head, and forgotten, folded hands;
> And at the foot of a grave a mother kneels
> With pale shut face, nor either hears nor feels
>
> The coming of the chanting choristers
> Between the avenue of cypresses,
> The silence of the many villagers,
> The candle-flames beside the surplices.

There may be something, then, in what Geoffrey Grigson has said of Lawrence's poems: 'the stronger the emotion, the more defined the structure'. In other words, the looseness and staccato quality of most of his free verse does not come from pressure of feeling—the words forcing themselves down, impatient of constraint—but from sheer *lack* of motive or impulse; so that they are notes on, rather than transmutations of, sensations and moods. Or—and perhaps this is particularly true of the poems in *Pansies* (a cheeky twisting of *pensées*)—the strong impulse was there, but had already spent its main strength in the novels, and what remains are its marginal traces, fragmentary and undisciplined. Yet ten or a dozen of his poems transcend this hastiness, keep their energy, find their own form and have a fresh and memorable existence of their own—an existence which needs no deprecating or qualifying statements about Lawrence's major work as a novelist.

CHAPTER FIVE

T. S. Eliot

(b. 1888)

The growth in Eliot's poetry is from the 'light' sardonic verse of *Prufrock and other Observations,* through various aspects of negation ('Gerontion', 'The Waste Land', 'The Hollow Men') and spiritual exhaustion/elation ('Ash Wednesday'), to the philosophical certitude of the *Four Quartets*. The 'variety and complexity' which he has seen as the products of our time are reflected in this growth; it is, in fact, the growth of a mind and a sensibility, as significant as (though very different from) that of Yeats. The different aspects of his background and experience have contributed to this growth, and it is useful briefly to consider these aspects under five headings: Eliot as an American, an Englishman, a Christian, a scholar and a conservative. The five are revealed in Eliot the poet and critic.

Born in the Middle West, but of New England stock and educated in New England during his university years, Eliot's background is representatively American. In 1930, three years after he had become a British citizen, Eliot wrote:

> Of course, my people were northerners and New Englanders, and of course I have spent many years out of America altogether; but Missouri and the Mississippi have made a deeper impression on me than any other part of the world.

These two strands are apparent in 'The Dry Salvages' (one of the *Four Quartets*) which he published eleven years later;

in it, the sea references are all obviously to the New England coast, and the river references just as obviously draw on the Mississippi-Missouri. In his early work, of course, the Americanism is linguistically more conspicuous, in such a term as 'butt-ends' in 'Prufrock', where the British equivalent would be 'cigarette-ends' or 'fag-ends'. But the culture of which Eliot was a part in his youth was, after all, orientated towards Europe; New England, and Boston in particular, is often jokingly called more English than England. It was natural, then, that Eliot should become one of that not very rare type, the American cultural *émigré*, not in the manner of Gertrude Stein or Hemingway, but more closely resembling that of Henry James and Ezra Pound. The particular sophistication, and the particular duality, of the cultural *émigré* are seen in 'Gerontion', 'Burbank with a Baedeker, Bleistein with a Cigar', the Sweeney poems and 'Sweeney Agonistes'; very different social commentaries from the specifically American 'The Boston Evening Transcript', 'Aunt Helen' and 'Cousin Nancy'. The clash is between the beautiful and the sordid, between the peak of a tradition and its decline; for example, in the Burbank-Bleistein poem, Venice has sunk from its former elegance and importance to the levels of commercialism and tourism. It is another facet of Henry James's Italy.

Indeed, the world of Eliot's earliest published poems is partly that of James, evident in the conversational cadences of 'Prufrock' and 'Portrait of a Lady'. The theme of both poems is inadequacy, and the particular ironical inadequacy which comes from the juxtaposition of the young and the old; in 'Prufrock', the prematurely middle-aged man among the young women, and in 'Portrait of a Lady', the young man and the older woman. There is bewilderment and misunderstanding, just as there is in the Sweeney poems, where we see the mingling of 'the horror and the boredom and the glory' which Eliot says the poet must find under all beauty and ugliness.

Eliot as an Englishman and a Christian has found a tradition and a meaning which were lacking when he was rootless. 'The Waste Land' (the main setting of which is London), 'The Hollow Men' and 'Ash Wednesday' show his gradual progression towards stability and faith; his first two plays, *The Rock* and *Murder in the Cathedral*, show his religious preoccupations at work in a dramatic, historical and social setting. The progress was a difficult one, relying on the will rather than the emotions; in the words of the first section of 'Ash Wednesday'

> Consequently I rejoice, having to construct something
> Upon which to rejoice . . .

The sense of place, the need for roots—these themes of Yeats are also Eliot's concerns, particularly in the *Four Quartets*, where the philosophical certitude is rooted in actual places, three of them in England: Burnt Norton, East Coker and Little Gidding. When, in 1927, Eliot adopted British nationality, he embraced not only a new country, nor simply a particular religious denomination, but a tradition and a faith towards which he had for some time been implicitly moving.

His scholarship reveals itself in a wide and deep knowledge of the literatures of the world, which serves to reinforce his sense of tradition. Greek, Latin, Italian, French and German literature and philosophy are as easily available to him as English; and his early training in Sanskrit has given him an insight into Oriental philosophical thought. With this training, and with his natural inclinations, Dante, Sophocles and Virgil are as important and relevant to him as Shakespeare,

Donne, Dryden. There is probably no other important poet in English literature (apart from Milton) who has had such a broad, informed view of the humanities. Thus it is that the sheer mass of assumed *knowledge* in 'The Waste Land' makes the approach difficult for even a moderately well-read reader: Ovid and the Upanishads, to take only two examples, are outside the general field of twentieth century Western reference. Yet they are part of the Tradition, the central stream of human experience, however much that stream may have been diverted. And it is his determination to keep the continuity of the Tradition which makes Eliot a conservative. In a perhaps deliberately provocative remark in 1928, he said that his tastes were 'classicist in literature, Anglo-Catholic in religion, royalist in politics'. It is because of this apparently rigid orthodoxy that he has sometimes been labelled 'reactionary' (there was his refusal, for example, to sign a manifesto declaring sympathy with the Republicans during the Spanish Civil War—when Eliot was almost alone in his uncommitted attitude), but he has never been bigoted or dogmatic; as a Director of Faber and Faber, he did, after all, publish the work of two of the chief so-called 'leftist' poets of the 1930s—Auden and Spender; and he has never been simply a supporter of the *status quo*. In his book *After Strange Gods* (some stimulating, but sometimes irritating, lectures delivered in America in 1933), he said:

> Tradition by itself is not enough; it must be perpetually criticised and brought up to date under the supervision of what I call orthodoxy . . . Most 'defenders of tradition' are mere conservatives, unable to distinguish between the permanent and the temporary, the essential and the accidental.

Eliot has since suppressed this book, probably because he feels that this particular application of orthodoxy at that time was hasty and capable of misinterpretation; but I think one is justified in regarding the passage I have just quoted as representative of his considered opinion. It is, after all, only saying in a more direct way what he continues to reprint in 'Tradition and the Individual Talent.'

Any reader of Eliot's poetry must regard his criticism as a necessary complement, outlining the purposes which direct, and the bases which underlie, the poetry. Eliot has always been deeply aware of the interrelation of the two, and this is especially apparent in 'Tradition and the Individual Talent' and 'The Use of Criticism'; indeed, if we add to these two a third essay, 'The Metaphysical Poets', we have a miniature guide to Eliot's critical precept and poetic practice.

So to the poems themselves, among which 'The Waste Land' and the *Four Quartets* are the most important. Both are, in a sense, 'musical' poems, in the way that certain central themes are repeated with variations; their structure is one of deliberate patterns, though the patterns in the *Four Quartets* are much more obvious than in 'The Waste Land'.

'The Waste Land' is often regarded as being primarily a reflection of twentieth century disillusionment and despair, and of course it does include these elements; hence its success as a 'universal' poem, translated into many languages and influential in the work of many poets. In Japan, for example, it is published in at least seven different translations, and 'wasturando' is a common enough word in modern Japanese criticism, denoting a whole area of westernised literary form and content. Yet it has a more particular meaning (if one can talk about 'The Waste Land's' definable 'meaning'), a pointer to which is given in the first part of the notes Eliot provided for the poem. The two books to which he refers (*From Ritual to Romance* and *The Golden Bough*) are studies of anthropological myth. Dealing with the first book, George Williamson says:

> . . . the experience of sex . . . assumes a universal or religious significance; it is connected with the state of the land. For the Vegetation myths erect the cycle of the seasons into a series of divinely ordered events; and this cycle of life is based on sex and personified in ritualistic figures. The fortune of the land depends upon the treatment of these figures, and thus upon religion.

But the world of 'The Waste Land' is one in which faith in 'divinely ordered events', and hence 'ritualistic figures', has been lost; there is sterility instead of fertility, waste instead of order. And this loss is ironically put in terms of prehistoric and primitive myths, thrown into contrast with conflicting images from past literature, from fragments of songs and scriptures (both Christian and non-Christian), from history and from modern life.

Thus the subject is really a religious one—the growth and decline of religious feeling in man—seen within the structure or framework of primitive ritualistic sex. The change of seasons, the beginning of new growth, is seen from the start as something painful, because man is now not capable of an adequate response:

> April is the cruellest month, breeding
> Lilacs out of the dead land, mixing
> Memory and desire, stirring
> Dull roots with spring rain . . .

'Memory and desire' are two of the many forces in opposition in 'The Waste Land'. Pangs of nostalgia (the hyacinth girl in Part 1, 'the pleasant whining of a mandoline' in Part 3, the boat in Part 5) jostle with memories of horror and emptiness (the encounter with Stetson in Part 1, 'I remember / Those are pearls that were his eyes' in Part 2, the songs of the three Thames Daughters in Part 3). But the memories are fragmentary and essentially meaningless; they form no coherent tradition; they are 'broken images'.

The force of 'The Waste Land' naturally cannot be extracted from one section alone, and there are many commentaries available which elucidate the poem as a whole. But it may be useful to consider here the particular *manner* of one part, Part 2, 'A Game of Chess'. In Part 1, the land is seen as barren; now, in Part 2, attention is concentrated on the sterility of *human* life. The section begins with an opulent description of the room of a rich woman, recalling Cleopatra and Dido; both have a reputation for being great lovers, great courtesans, out of an historical and almost mythical past. But the modern woman in the poem exists in the middle of sterile splendour; for example, the Cupidon (love-god) is, ironically, golden—an expensive ornament, with no living significance to the woman. The descriptive lines (77–96) are like something from a Jacobean play, with all the baroque richness of such a dramatist as Ben Jonson (compare the description of wealth in *Volpone*) but, as in Jonson, the lavishness of verbal ornamentation serves to emphasise miserliness. In this setting, even the exquisite cries of Philomel, pursued by Tereus, have come to be debased to 'Jug Jug'; she is the nightingale in the desert, the glimpse of forgotten beauty in the waste land. At this point, the narrative moves from description to an impressionistic treatment of nightmare figures, symbols of the rich woman's neurosis, and the woman brushes her hair into sparks which

Glowed into words, then would be savagely still.

The dialogue which follows is a mutually self-enclosed one between the woman and her husband or lover. The woman's words are harsh, abrupt, repetitive: the man's replies are ironical, sardonic, giving nothing away. The eyes of 'the drowned Phoenician Sailor' of Part 1 (who re-appears as the central figure in Part 4) serve only as the background to a jazzy tune in the head, perverting Shakespeare's Ariel dirge from *The Tempest*. The woman's hysteria grows, yet her repeated emphasis on nullity (notice the repetition of 'nothing' five times in lines 120–123) leads to a plain statement of fact—

> The hot water at ten.
> And if it rains, a closed car at four . . .

the complete emptiness of the life which these people lead, with behind it an inexplicable and indescribable menace— 'a knock upon the door'.

The immediate juxtaposition of the working-class scene in the pub heightens the contrast. Here is a world where human beings are sexually fecund, but that very fecundity is wasteful, and drives them to their death. The 'knock upon the door' is not something in the distant future, waiting at the end of almost interminable boredom, but a present reality, implicit in the gruff tones of the publican calling out closing-time in the pub: 'HURRY UP PLEASE ITS TIME'. The scene is localised, both in time and place, much more closely than any other in the poem; the gossip about Lil and Albert is definitely set in the post-First World War period, and in a London pub; the language is fairly accurately reported Cockney. Sex is seen loosely as having 'a good time', but sex of this sort is as empty as sterility. The attempts at self-induced abortion ('It's them pills I took, to bring it off . . . The chemist said it would be all right, but I've never been the same') lead simply to a premature ageing. Yet despite the fear and emptiness of these people's lives, there is a basic rightness somewhere under their crude attitudes—'What you get married for if you don't want children?' Rather like the 'Proles' in Orwell's *1984*, they serve as a fitting contrast to 'the other world'—the world of arid boredom. They at least have their roots, however withered, in some code of conduct which has a direct relation to life. Their trivial farewells merge into the words of Ophelia's farewell in her 'mad scene' (*Hamlet*, Act 4, Scene 5)—words which follow on from her 'and so I thank you for your good counsel.' Lou's and May's advice to Lil is harsh and insensitive; but it has the heart of the matter in it.

This is a synopsis, not an analysis, of the section, and of course there are many other undertones and links which could be commented on; to take only one example, the connection with the woman in Part 5 who 'drew her long black hair out tight' in the nightmare passage of 'voices singing out of empty cisterns and exhausted wells'—the sterile splendour of Part 2 reinforces the sterility of the 'decayed hole among the mountains' where stands the 'empty chapel', once the home of the Grail (the chapel is in fact the Chapel Perilous) which could, in the Arthurian legends, bring life, through Christ's blood, to men. Here the primitive fertility myths and Christianity are fused, and the continuity of religious experience is shown.

'The Waste Land' is thus not a mere reflection of hopelessness but a panoramic view of spiritual exhaustion, comparable in desolation to the 'terrible' sonnets of Hopkins. The soul is scoured, and waits in emptiness for its revival. This aspect of Christian mysticism is developed in 'Ash Wednesday', published eight years later. The soul in this poem is

> Wavering between the profit and the loss
> In this brief transit where the dreams cross
> The dreamcrossed twilight between birth and dying . . .

It must move through a sort of earthly purgatory before it can be refined into 'the higher love' (i.e. of God); it must renounce the world, and indeed has ceased to expect anything of it ('I no longer strive to strive towards such things'); but it is not yet able to embrace anything else. Like Arnaut Daniel in Dante's *Purgatorio*, the poet dives into 'the refining fire' (it is worth pointing out that this line—'Poi s'ascose nel foco che gli affina'— is from one of the passages in Dante which has most moved Eliot's imagination; it is used in the final section of 'The Waste Land'; and the first words of Daniel's petition ('Ara vos prec'—'Now I pray you') served as the title for his 1920 volume of poems, which included 'Gerontion'—another purgatorial meditation. To those of us who cannot read Italian, Eliot's own essay on Dante is a useful crib—for the purpose of appreciating Eliot, if not Dante).

The poet calls out of the depths, where the air is

> . . . thoroughly small and dry
> Smaller and dryer than the will.

All that is left is the possibility of death, and it is out of that fact that he turns to 'construct something / Upon which to rejoice.' Part 2 leads to the conclusion that death has at least made quiet the flesh's desires (the bones' prophecy is all that is left of them). Part 3 begins the ascent out of the depths, passing the images of decayed old age ('Damp, jagged, like an old man's mouth drivelling, beyond repair') and the enticements of youth ('Blown hair is sweet, brown hair over the mouth blown'). The Lady, who appears vaguely in Part 2, merges into the figure of Mary the Virgin in Part 4, where she connects the old life which he has renounced and the new life which he is not yet ready to receive; Mary unites the earthly and the divine. The movement is towards 'the higher dream', the supreme expression of Love. But nothing is yet certain;

> The silent sister veiled in white and blue
> Between the yews, behind the garden god,
> Whose flute is breathless, bent her head and signed but spoke no
>   word . . .

The revelation of the Word made flesh (God's appearance in Christ) follows in Part 5, but is deliberately muffled at first in a confused passage which revolves round the words 'Word', 'world', 'whirled', 'unheard' and 'unspoken'; the revelation is not meant to be a clear, straightforward awareness of truth, but a sharper realisation of the *dilemma*—the difficulty of choice between the 'higher' and the 'lower' love.

In Part 6, the poem turns from this confusion (which yet contains the possibility of clarity) and recapitulates, in slightly different form, the words with which the poem began. But now the significant word is 'Although', not 'Because'—the fact of hope is conceded, not denied. As in the confessional (hence 'Bless me father'), the things of the world are acknowledged to have their grip on him, but he can renounce them and can testify that, beyond them, 'Our peace (is) in His will' (another echo from Dante). Throughout the poem, sentences from the Bible and the Prayer Book outline the struggle between the opposing forces in the poet's will; and the last section is a direct petition, through the Virgin Mary, asking for the guidance of a God whom he now accepts; the last line is the Prayer Book response to the words, 'O Lord hear our prayer.' Spiritual death has been overcome, and contact with God is possible.

The *Four Quartets* are a natural development and expansion, in some ways, of 'Ash Wednesday', but the main points are more easily grasped, because the spiritual progress moves through time and space and is not simply seen in a sort of mystical reverie. Also, the poem is not one of struggle but acceptance; and there is a cohesion in the structure which was deliberately lacking in 'Ash Wednesday'. Nevertheless, I must not suggest that the *Four Quartets* are in any sense more easily paraphrasable than the other poems; they are not, and when I say 'the main points' I mean something relatively limited. It is a help, for example, to take the hint, given by several critics, that each of the Quartets is concerned with a basic element—air in 'Burnt Norton', earth in 'East Coker', water in 'The Dry Salvages' and fire in 'Little Gidding'. These are the four elements which constitute life. The total subject of the poem can be said to be the unity to which all four contribute, but since that unity is—as I have indicated—life itself, we are really not much nearer a satisfactory definition. It is perhaps better to approach it in the way we read Wordsworth's *The Prelude*—as a poem which, very roughly, is about 'the growth of a poet's mind'. And just as *The Prelude* contains much material which is incidental or subordinate to this generalisation, so in the *Four Quartets* we see a mind ranging over personal experiences, over history and the present time, over the struggles of poetry and the difficulties of language, over the sense of place and the sense of time. Though the poem has a fine formal beauty, there is no unified conclusion, no neat parcelling of relevant facts: in the words of the fifth section of 'Little Gidding'

> We shall not cease from exploration
> And the end of our exploring
> Will be to arrive where we started
> And know the place for the first time.

And both the method and the meaning are touched on in these lines from the fifth section of 'The Dry Salvages':

> These are only hints and guesses,
> Hints followed by guesses; and the rest
> Is prayer, observance, discipline, thought and action.
> The hint half guessed, the gift half understood, is Incarnation.

So 'the word made Flesh' in Part 5 of 'Ash Wednesday', in the midst of doubt and confusion, is the central reality in the *Four Quartets*; 'half guessed . . . half understood', but still a reality. In this, both time and place are given meaning:

> Here the impossible union
> Of spheres of existence is actual,
> Here the past and the future
> Are conquered, and reconciled . . .

But 'For most of us, this is the aim / Never here to be realised.' When I said, at the beginning of this essay, that Eliot reached 'philosophical certitude' in the *Four Quartets*, I did not mean that he felt he had solved all the puzzles or answered all the questions; faith does not necessarily entirely preclude doubt. When we say, in ordinary speech, that someone has taken his bad luck 'philosophically', we mean that there is enough stability in the man (and hence enough faith) to withstand whatever has happened to him. This is a kind of certitude perhaps stronger than any unquestioning acceptance: 'Lord, I believe: help thou my unbelief.' Those words from St. Mark's Gospel might serve as an epigraph to the whole of Eliot's poetry, where the triumph is in the reconciliation of opposites,

> . . . restored by that refining fire
> Where you must move in measure, like a dancer.

CHAPTER SIX

W. H. Auden

(b. 1907)

To those who look for 'high seriousness' in poetry, as
Matthew Arnold looked for it in Chaucer and found it
lacking, Auden will not be a satisfactory poet. Robert
Graves, for instance, has dismissed him by saying 'his real
talent . . . is for light verse.' And Auden himself has said
in his *Letter to Lord Byron*

> You must ask me who
> Have written just as I'd have liked to do.
> I stop to listen and the names I hear
> Are those of Firbank, Potter, Carroll, Lear.

He has edited the *Oxford Book of Light Verse*; he has written
light ballads (using light treatment of ugly, and even cruel,
subjects) such as 'Miss Gee' and 'James Honeyman'; humorous
conversational verse, such as the *Letter to Lord Byron* quoted
above; satirical and sentimental songs, such as the one which
begins

> You were a great Cunarder, I
> Was only a fishing smack.
> Once you passed across my bows
> And of course you did not look back.

Yet though these things are obvious in Auden's work, and
though many of them are extremely successful within their

prescribed limits, they do not form the central stream of his poetry. Auden himself realises this, for when he came to issue his *Collected Shorter Poems* he ruthlessly rejected many of his 'light' pieces; and most of those that were left he put in a separate section at the end of the book—'Songs and other musical pieces.'

The more important question is the lightness of *tone* in many of the other poems—poems which are obviously meant to be considered seriously, and not as mere 'entertainments'. (It is interesting here to note Graham Greene's division of his books into 'novels' and 'entertainments'.) With Eliot we are aware of a tone which is almost wholly serious; Kenneth Allott makes the point that when Eliot writes light verse, as in *Old Possum's Book of Practical Cats*, we feel that it is rather like an eminent and respectable uncle unbending at a party for his little nephews and nieces, playing the fool for half an hour. We feel, too, that at the end of that half-hour he will once again become eminent and respectable, though in the meantime the children (and the uncle) enjoy the fun. With Auden, on the other hand, there is no such air of condescension. Instead, there is a kind of wit—adult, sophisticated, and sometimes obscure; a wit that relies on statements of epigrammatic conciseness and on metaphors and similes where ideas, 'yoked by violence together', amaze one with their audacity (or, sometimes, annoy one with their irrelevance). And the strange thing is that Auden manages to combine this witty tone, very often, with a note of urgent warning or impending doom. The message is made more telling by the hint of a sardonic smile in the background. Take, for instance, the second sonnet in his sequence *The Quest*. The point of this poem is that man is in a constant state of apprehension, and thus arms himself with paraphernalia with which to combat, or survive, any possible situation; and yet man's apprehension springs from a situation *within himself*, which cannot be dealt with by any outward means. The lesson is 'Physician, heal thyself'—not with medicine (physical or spiritual), but by becoming, in a favourite quotation of Auden's, 'pure in heart'. Auden is here preaching a moral sermon, and—like many preachers—he uses a parable to illustrate his meaning. The human race is seen as a band of explorers about to go into unknown territory; they order their equipment and lay in supplies for every contingency—'instruments', 'drugs', 'a watch', 'lamps', 'shades', 'a gun', 'coloured beads' with which to mollify the natives. But it is no use, because by so carefully preparing for possible 'situations' (situations which may in fact never arise) they are deceiving themselves, not seeing that they are 'their (own) situation'. The paraphernalia is simply a handy, but specious, cure for their own condition. And in the last three lines Auden obliquely emphasises this by pointing out three analogous cases:

> One should not give a poisoner medicine,
> A conjurer fine apparatus, nor
> A rifle to a melancholic bore.

It can be seen from those three lines how light the tone is; yet the lightness is not one of triviality, but of the surgeon who knows just how delicate and dangerous is the operation he is about to perform, and nevertheless makes a wry joke as he goes into the operating theatre. The comparison to a surgeon is indeed relevant to Auden; Auden treats his main subject-matter—human beings—clinically. ('Clinical' is another favourite term of his.) This clinical humour can be seen in its starkest form, having more in common with the cruel jokes of a raw young medical-student than with a surgeon, in his ballad 'Miss Gee', where the spinster's psychological inhibitions and physiological cancer are seen to have a direct connection, and both of them are seen in a heartlessly funny light.

Richard Hoggart has pointed out how important the word 'Love' is in Auden's poetry. Probably his most famous single line is

> We must love one another or die.

Yet it is often difficult to tell exactly what he means by it. It is obviously not simply meant in a sexual sense, nor does it cover 'deep regard for one's fellow men'. Except in a few later poems, it is not love of God. Looking through the *Collected Shorter Poems*, almost at random, one comes across example after example:

1. O *Love*, the interest itself in thoughtless Heaven,
   Make simpler daily the beating of man's heart . . .

2. These moods give no permission to be idle,
   For men are changed by what they do;
   And through loss and anger the hands of the unlucky
   Love one another.

3. O can you see precisely in our gaucheness
   The neighbour's strongest wish, to serve and *love*?

4. For the error bred in the bone
   Of each woman and each man
   Craves what it cannot have,
   Not universal *love*
   But to be *loved* alone.

5. And lived expensively and did without,
   And could not find the earth which he had paid for,
   Nor feel the *love* that he knew all about.

6.   O stand, stand at the window
     As the tears scald and start;
     You shall *love* your crooked neighbour
     With your crooked heart.

And yet Auden is not, in the sense that Yeats was, a love poet, at any rate in the normal usage of that term. The only satisfactory poem of his addressed to a loved one is 'Lay your sleeping head, my love.' One senses no strong personal feeling of love in Auden, as one does in the individual cynicism of Donne and the individual violence of Yeats. Nor is there much feeling of warm compassion; the clinical atmosphere precludes that.

What then, is this 'love'? I would express it, tentatively, like this: it is the central dogma in Auden's personal theology, a theology which (even in his non-Christian period— roughly, from his adolescence until he was about 36) has been strongly influenced by Christian thought. Just as the Christian (especially the Roman Catholic) has a notion of Grace as a sort of reservoir into which is poured each drop of prayer, so Auden thinks of man's individual and unselfish good acts in relation to Love. Auden himself, in a poem which admirably unites lightness of tone with seriousness of purpose ('Law Like Love'), has admitted how difficult it is to define this idea, or indeed any idea about love. The poem, for most of its length, is ostensibly saying something about the word, or the idea of, Law. The gardeners say it is one thing, the old another thing, the young yet another thing, the priest something else; judges, scholars, and many others give their personal interpretations. And that is the point— all their intrepretations are *personal*, biased, self-interested. Having shown this, Auden turns to consider Love, which is similarly lost among individual interpretations and definitions;

and, having also shown how 'absurd' it is 'To identify Law with some other word', he realises that it is as impossible to say firmly 'Love is such-and-such' as it is to say firmly 'Law is such-and-such.' All that we can do is put forward some 'timid similarity', tentatively saying that Love is as ignorant, powerless, sad and transient as the rest of the human condition:

> Like love we don't know where or why
> Like love we can't compel or fly
> Like love we often weep
> Like love we seldom keep.

'Law Like Love' is one of Auden's gentlest and most wistful poems. Elsewhere he is much more ready to be assured and definitive; and it is significant that Love, which I have shown is such a central idea in his work, is treated less dogmatically, more mysteriously, than any other of his themes. If one can make a bold generalisation about Auden, it is this; everything he writes is concerned, above all, with 'the human element'. A large part of his poetry is directly about human behaviour, rules of conduct, the clash of the abnormal with the normal, and the definition of all these. It has been said that Auden's concern is with 'maps and chaps' (that is, places and people); but the maps, the landscapes, the urban scenes, are there simply as a background for human beings. Auden seems to stand above the world, and surveys it (in the words of one of his early poems) 'As the hawk sees it or the helmeted airman'. And what he sees is human aspiration, human misery, human deception and self-deception, human progress and human reaction. He does not describe these things; he defines them. G. S. Fraser says, 'He diagnoses a disease and suggests a remedy', but I think a close reading of

his poems will show that his greater energies go into making
the diagnosis; the remedy, when he does seem to suggest one,
can be expressed in a simple imperative, three simple words:
'Be perfectly honest.' This rather crude simplification of
mine can be applied equally well to Freud and to Auden.
Indeed, Freud (together with three other psychologists,
personally known to Auden—George Groddeck, Homer
Lane and John Layard) has had a powerful influence on
Auden's thought. Perfect honesty (which necessitates both
lack of inhibition and lack of self-deception) is the lesson of
Freud's which Auden has taken most to heart. As he wrote
in his fine poem 'In Memory of Sigmund Freud':

> He wasn't clever at all: he merely told
> The unhappy Present to recite the Past
> Like a poetry lesson till sooner
> Or later it faltered at the line where
> Long ago the accusations had begun . . .

And having unburdened ourselves of those things which,
unknown to us, had been weighing us down with guilt or
anxiety or fear, we are

> Able to approach the Future as a friend
> Without a wardrobe of excuses, without
> A set mask of rectitude or an
> Embarrassing over-familiar gesture.

Obviously, this 'remedy' is purely an individual one; the
great mass of man cannot be brought under psychoanalysis,
useful and healthful though Auden would consider it to be.
Man, through the centuries a creature of great potentialities,
has grown to have great power, great knowledge and great
numbers; yet, says Auden, despite the fact that he has constructed all the sciences and all the arts, has developed the

power of abstract thought and of manufacturing every material thing he needs, has covered the earth with his houses and his schemes—despite all this, he is sick and unhappy. It is an idea which he deals with succinctly and typically in sonnet number VIII from his sequence *In Time of War*. The sickness here is not a Freudian one of individual dishonesty and self-deception; it is a *social* sickness, of man as a mass. Throughout the poem, man is simply 'he', a third person whom we can see individually and in retrospect. In the first line,

> He turned his field into a meeting-place,

we immediately grasp the point that this 'he' is a convenient way of saying 'all of us', and each line adds a little more to this generalised picture. Each line, too, is a unit in itself, so that when we have read the poem we have seen fourteen different stages in the process of man's degeneration and dis-enchantment. Man, the individual farmer, becomes a social being, involved in trade, government and conversation; rubbing against his fellows, he becomes tolerant and easy-going, losing his strict personal standards; he wishes to make profits and be liked, both at the same time. He has a vague idea that men are equal, and should be treated with equality, but when he is confronted by strangers he hardly sees them—their faces merely have a mechanical meaning to him. He builds, so that the sky is thick with his own creation; he shuts away the knowledge and art of centuries, knowing (for no good reason) that it ought to be kept, but having no real use for it. All the economic factors which govern him are no more than bits of paper—whether bank-notes or bureaucratic forms. All these things

> grew so fast his life was overgrown;

he no longer knows why he is on earth or what the earth means to him; he becomes part of the mass, to find comfort in numbers, and finds that he is more alone than ever; he squanders and he saves. In the end the earth, which at first was in a very real sense his own (though he knew only a limited part of it), is now out of his control—though, paradoxically, he has spent centuries in mastering it. And Love, which we have seen is, in Auden's view, man's primary emotion (though often misdirected or perverted), has become something which he knows 'all about' *in theory*, but which he cannot experience *in fact*. Every facet and nuance of Love is familiar to him theoretically, from Plato's *Symposium* to theological works on *eros* and *agape*, and from the great love poetry of the world to Hollywood on the one hand and Dr. Kinsey on the other; but it is all in his head, not in his heart.

Marxism, which to many people has seemed the answer to the problems of man as a social being, influenced Auden for some time, though he was never a communist. He simply saw, or thought he saw, an historical process which was inevitable and from which one could not escape. This certainty appears in many of his poems of the 1930s, and is perhaps most energetically expressed in the poem which opens, 'Since you are going to begin today', and which ends with these lines:

> Do not imagine you can abdicate;
> Before you reach the frontier you are caught;
> Others have tried it and will try again
> To finish that which they did not begin:
> Their fate must always be the same as yours,
> To suffer the loss they were afraid of, yes,
> Holders of one position, wrong for years.

The landscape over which this struggle is fought is a strange one, peculiarly Auden's own; it is, in John Lehmann's words,

> A world which seems to be in the throes of a strange guerilla campaign with secret conspiracies on all sides; dangerous frontiers to unknown countries which have to be crossed or not crossed; doom and catastrophe; the countryside is generally mountainous and apt to be filled with industrial ruins.

This Audenesque landscape is, geographically, a mixture of two actual landscapes: that of the Lake District, the fells and moorland of Cumberland and Westmorland which Auden knew so well from his childhood and youth, an area of bleak beauty—an 'austere' beauty, to use another of his favourite words; and that of the industrial Midlands and the industrial North, which during the Depression of the early 1930s were places of

> Smokeless chimneys, damaged bridges, rotting wharves and
>   choked canals,
> Tramlines buckled, smashed trucks lying on their sides across
>   the rails.

Yet, as I have said before, for Auden this multiple landscape is simply a background for man, for the human situation. In *Letter to Lord Byron* he wrote:

> To me art's subject is the human clay,
> And landscape but the background to a torso.

Even in his later work, much of which is ostensibly about different geographical features (such as the series of poems called 'Mountains', 'Lakes', 'Islands', 'Plains' and so on), the concern is the same; 'Mountains', for example, is almost

wholly about the reactions of specific types to mountains—
'a retired dentist', great painters, 'those unsmiling parties/
Clumping off at dawn', 'the boy behind his goats', and
(obliquely) Auden himself.

Though I have said that Marxism 'influenced Auden for
some time' in his search for the answer to man's plight as a
social being, he never absorbed it enough—or perhaps never
took it seriously enough—to make it an integral part of his
poetry. His most consistently Marxist piece is *The Dance of
Death*, an early dramatic satire in light charade form. In it,
Marx himself appears, and is seen at the end as a logically
inevitable but also rather a comic figure. When the Dancer,
who represents the death of western civilisation, is eventually
revealed to be dead himself, the Chorus sings (in the manner
of a popular song):

> O Mr. Marx you've gathered
> All the material facts,
> You know the economic
> Reasons for our acts.

and Marx enters, flanked by two young communists, to
announce of the Dancer: 'The instruments of production
have been too much for him. He is liquidated.' The lightness
of tone here is not the lightness of 'Law Like Love'; it is
trivial and rather embarrassing. One feels like asking, 'If
Auden could treat this business in such a silly manner, did
he really feel strongly about it?' The answer is twofold. He
was much more interested in the symbolical struggle in a
landscape of 'abandoned lead-mines' and 'snatches of tramline'
than he was in the day-to-day achievement of doctrinaire
Marxism—the world of (as he expressed it) 'the flat ephemeral
pamphlet and the boring meeting'; and, despite all his

generalised pictures, he was more concerned with the individual than with the mass. One can see why Auden described himself as seen by his communist friends as 'a selfish pink old Liberal to the last'.

Auden, therefore, never committed himself politically, unlike Day Lewis and Spender. On the other hand he has always been aware of, and a disciple of, what he has very often called 'Order'. He has always believed that men have an instinctive desire to lead (again in his own words) 'The Good Life', but that they are frustrated, partly by their own innate evil and partly by their own selfish rebellion against necessity. This is the central theme of one of his most important later poems, written in America, *New Year Letter*:

> How grandly would our virtues bloom
> In a more conscionable dust
> Where Freedom dwells because it must
> Necessity because it can,
> And men confederate in Man.

These things will be achieved, says Auden, by Order: and what he means by Order is something closely analogous to Love. In 'Canzone', another later poem, he says

> we are required to love
> All homeless objects that require a world.

These 'homeless objects' are men; and just as in his early, non-Christian poem 'The Malverns' he asserted that

> through loss and anger the hands of the unlucky
> Love one another,

so here, in these Christian poems, he says that it is men's duty to make the lives of their fellows more bearable. In an interesting essay published in 1948, which Richard Hoggart quotes, Auden wrote:

> If the Good Samaritan is asked why he rescued the man who fell among thieves, he may answer: 'because I like doing good'; but the answer will be a joking reproof to the interrogator for asking silly questions when he already knows the answer, which is, that to love one's neighbour as oneself is an order, and whether I enjoy obeying an order or not is irrelevant.

I have said that these later poems are Christian; Auden's acceptance that 'to love one's neighbour as oneself is an order' is the acceptance of a Christian. It therefore follows that it is God whose orders require man to achieve Order and Love. He has given man free-will, so that man can choose, but He has not necessarily given him either the strength or the conscience to achieve *what* he chooses; the strength and the conscience must be asked for. This is the meaning of the splendid invocation towards the end of *New Year Letter*:

> O Voice
> Within the labyrinth of choice . . .
> Disturb our negligence and chill,
> Convict our pride of its offence
> In all things, even penitence,
> Instruct us in the civil art
> Of making from the muddled heart
> A desert and a city where
> The thoughts that have to labour there
> May find locality and peace,
> And pent-up feelings their release.
> Send strength sufficient for our day,
> And point our knowledge on its way,
> *O da quod jubes, Domine.*

'Give what You have commanded, O Lord.' Marxian Necessity, which Auden saw but could not really help to achieve, has become Christian Order, in which he feels himself to be an active member, achieving as well as seeing.

Yet it must not be thought that there are two Audens—in glib phraseology, 'the left-wing intellectual' and 'the Christian intellectual'. The development is clearly marked and consistent, and one feels that there is a wholeness in Auden rather than a division. If one senses a slackness and general unsatisfactoriness in some of Auden's later poems, one should not too quickly ascribe this to 'a change of belief'. The faults are mainly technical, faults of a man who has always experimented widely and with varying success. He has been a prolific writer since his very early days, and prolific writers are always in danger of writing work which is dull, careless and inflated; consider Wordsworth, Byron, Tennyson. I feel that those who severely criticise Auden's recent work are, on the whole, correct; but I cannot agree with anyone who says, on the evidence of that work, that Auden is finished as an important poet. To close with an example, these lines from 'The Shield of Achilles', a poem in his most recent book, should silence any such judgment:

> The mass and majesty of this world, all
> That carries weight and always weighs the same,
> Lay in the hands of others; they were small
> And could not hope for help, and no help came;
> What their foes liked to do was done; their shame
> Was all the worst could wish: they lost their pride
> And died as men before their bodies died.

CHAPTER SEVEN

Spender, MacNeice and Day Lewis

The three poets with which this chapter is concerned have always been associated with Auden in the public mind; they are all about the same age, came from similar middle-class professional backgrounds, were contemporaries or near-contemporaries at Oxford after a public school education, and were all, in varying degrees of committedness, politically engaged in a direction which one can loosely call 'Left'. Roy Campbell, who vigorously despised most things they have done and written, lumped them together as a composite figure—'Macspaunday'. But they cannot so easily be classified. Auden is quite obviously the dominant figure, from whom all the others have learned, and his talents are far more rich and various than theirs. Yet Spender, MacNeice and Day Lewis have written enough independently interesting work to justify giving a chapter to them.

The viewpoints from which they started writing in the early 1930s have been outlined by Stephen Spender in his autobiography, *World Within World*:

> Perhaps . . . the qualities which distinguished us from the writers of the previous decade lay not in ourselves, but in the events to which we reacted. These were unemployment, economic crisis, nascent fascism, approaching war . . .

1920-30 was, from the literary point of view, an unpolitical decade. Yet they were years of tremendous political upheaval and social change. In 1922, Mussolini had come to power in Italy; in 1926 the General Strike paralysed Britain; in 1929, there was the Wall Street crash and similar financial chaos in Europe during the early 1930s, resulting in widespread unemployment. Those poets who had fought in the war—Sassoon and Blunden, for example—recoiled from the post-war mess and withdrew into contemplative gentleness. Wilfred Owen, who might have found material in this new kind of misery, was dead. Edith Sitwell was, in the popular mind, the leader of the 1920s *avant garde*, and her verbal fantasies, such as *Façade*, took no notice whatever of the social miseries of the time. It was left to the generation whose childhood had been spent during the war to face the facts and to attempt to make them into literature—a literature of protest and warning.

Spender (b.1909) has been called 'the Rupert Brooke of the Depression', a phrase which chiefly draws attention to the fact that both Brooke and Spender resemble the popular romantic ideal of what a poet should look like. They have little else in common, apart from an occasional over-ripeness of language (more common in Brooke than in Spender). Spender has shown in *World Within World* how, coming from a nineteenth century Liberal family of politicians and editors, he rebelled against his background but carried its rather muddled humanitarianism into his own unorthodox brand of communism. The very title of his early political tract, *Forward From Liberalism*, shows the basis of his thought at this time. Yet his actual membership of the Communist Party lasted only a few months, for his sensitive and independent spirit could never be doctrinaire; he was always too willing, from the Party's point of view, to see both sides of the question, and too self-centred ever to be an adequate member of a revolutionary team.

His main concern has always been with pity, a clumsy but intuitive feeling for the weakness of man, and particularly of himself. He is thus a personal poet in a way Auden never is, MacNeice only in brief ironical passages, Day Lewis only in his later work (apart from sections of *From Feathers to Iron*, which I shall deal with later in this chapter). He has always been (in his own words) 'an autobiographer restlessly searching for forms in which to express the stages of my development'. Or, in his 'Darkness and Light',

> To break out of the chaos of my darkness
> Into a lucid day, is all my will.

Not all autobiographers are honest; but Spender always is. Indeed, one never doubts his honesty, though one may question his astuteness, his good sense and his taste. In his early poems, some of which must be considered his best, he often seems to be like a gauche and embarrassed child blurting out some private thought which he has only just put into words—waiting for the more sophisticated adults to laugh at him. John Lehmann, at his first meeting with Spender, 'found him the most rapidly self-revealing person' he had ever met, and self-revelation often seems either comic or weak (or both) to those with tougher sensibilities. When his pity turns from himself to the outside world, the glimpse of deep compassion is often lost in his vague, repetitive words, as if his mind were continually following a circuit back to himself. Thus, in 'The Prisoners', he is aware that his pity affects himself far more strongly than it does the prisoners:

> My pity moves amongst them like a breeze
> On walls of stone
> Fretting for summer leaves, or like a tune
> On ears of stone.

The repetition here is merely self-centred and self-indulgent.

In his early poems he also attempted new subjects, such as 'The Landscape near an Aerodrome' and 'The Express'. Both are interesting examples of attempts to make myths or allegories out of modern material, but in each the conclusion is spoiled—in the first by a heavy, obtrusive didacticism ('The Church stands blocking the sun') and in the second by worn-out poetic cliches (the railway express is seen as finer than 'bird song' or 'bough/Breaking with honey buds'). This inability satisfactorily to conclude a poem is a feature of some of Spender's work; perhaps it has something to do with lack of logical concentration—individual fine passages do not add up to a whole because of emotional incoherence. In 'The Landscape near an Aerodrome', the success is achieved wholly through the almost arbitrary impressionistic description; the shape of the poem is determined only by the spatial movement of the observer, who sees first the plane itself, then the town to which the plane descends, then looks back to the journey of which this is the end, then returns to a closer, but deliberately distorted, view of the industrial landscape where the plane lands. The description is oblique, even hysterical, and one feels that the scene is observed with the inward, rather than the outward, eye. In particular the third section twists the features of the landscape into the generalised horror of a nightmare; precise and loose images are carelessly juxtaposed. For example, 'lank black fingers', 'like women's faces / Shattered by grief' and 'like a dog / Shut out and shivering at the foreign moon' are precise, in varying degrees, whereas 'figures frightening and mad', 'buildings / With their strange air behind trees' and 'the unhomely sense of complaint' are loose; pictorially and emotionally, they add little to what has already been said. As for the last section, the implied condemnation of religion is too summarily dragged in; it is too late to give any moral shock, because there has been nothing in the rest of the poem to make such a statement (and thus such a shock) relevant.

During the Spanish Civil War, Spender visited Spain and aided the Republicans with a certain amount of propaganda work. The poems he wrote at this period were 'engaged', but only as far as his *personal* feelings would allow him; he was not a 'war-poet' in the usual sense of that term. In 'Fall of a City', for example, the basic emotion may seem to be close to Wilfred Owen, but the attitude is much more complex than anything in Owen; it sees the struggle as, in a sense, meaningless, but it also acknowledges the fact of bravery, of 'energy', something potentially good which may result from this destruction. But neither is seen explicitly. In 'Ultima Ratio Regum', he says, of a boy killed in the fighting,

> Ask. Was so much expenditure justified
> On the death of one so young and so silly
> Lying under the olive trees, O world, O death?

And in 'Two Armies' the actual combatants are seen as innocent and peaceful; it is only 'the furious words and minerals which destroy':

> Clean silence drops at night, when a little walk
> Divides the sleeping armies, each
> Huddled in linen woven by remote hands.
> When the machines are stilled, a common suffering
> Whitens the air with breath and makes both one
> As though these enemies slept in each other's arms.

At the same time, his first wife left him; and this, rather than the war, was perhaps the major shock of the poems of his middle period, out of which, paradoxically, came some of his best and most characteristic love poetry. These poems are not, as one might expect, self-pitying; rather, they are self-accusing, probing mercilessly his feelings of his own guilt and inadequacy. In 'The Double Shame', a typical poem on this theme, one is aware of a certain blurring of focus at first, a characteristic hesitancy and imprecision in such lines as

> Pull down the blind and lie on the bed
> And clasp the hour in the glass of one room
> Against your mouth like a crystal doom,

where 'a crystal doom' is particularly vague and inexplicable. But this is an instance of a poem in which Spender has managed to concentrate his energies in his conclusion:

> At first you did not love enough
> And afterwards you loved too much
> And you lacked the confidence to choose
> And you have only yourself to blame.

This is interesting partly for the way in which it shows how Spender's directness and honesty can often circumvent his technical clumsiness, and indeed give positive force to something which might otherwise be unremarkable; the first three lines are perfectly regular, but the fourth line's metre is jerky, with the jerkiness of conversational prose:

> And you have only yourself to blame.

Thus the steady beat of accusation in the first three statements is broken, and the harsh, crude, completely honest fourth statement is left to end the poem.

His poems since then have on the whole not been so interesting. The scale and range of the Second World War was too big for his restricted vision, and the work inspired by those years was not successful. He returned to personal themes with a series of sonnets, called 'Explorations', in 1944, and his sequence, 'Elegy for Margaret', shows some of his old simplicity of expression—sometimes betrayed into the banal and the merely 'poetic'. It is the general emotional slackness of his later work which one finds depressing. Yet Spender, on the record of his poems from 1930–39, is, I think, next to Auden in importance in the group. The poetry of the two is in many ways in opposition, or rather, it is complementary. Spender's is almost wholly that of the weak and the unsure, where that of Auden is strong and assured: Auden analyses and dissects, while Spender observes and broods. In Spender, I find in glimpses the real stuff of poetry—compassion, honesty, and the struggle with intractable material.

LOUIS MacNEICE

It is easy both to over-rate the poetry of Louis MacNeice (b. 1907) and to be patronising about it. His work is very readable, he is never boring, he is an excellent craftsman, and he has many of the virtues of a good journalist—a 'reporter of experience' with sharp, vivid, precise phrases. But he seldom has much depth or penetration, and his general lightness of tone is more that of the professional entertainer than it is with Auden. He has generally been at his best with colloquial and contemporary language and themes, and with quick snapshots of behaviour. Francis Scarfe, in *Auden and After*, calls his chapter on MacNeice 'Poetry and Common Sense', and that is certainly the first quality one grants to him as a poet; he observes the objective, political, man-made world with great clarity and common-sense awareness, which has prevented him from ever being committed to any particular dogma; he was never caught up by communism, but stood on the edge, observing ironically, even at times cynically. His participation, then and now, stops at knowing all the facts (which Spender would never bother to do); having known them, he is disillusioned. Thus in 'Autumn Journal', a long discursive poem which he wrote at the time of the Munich crisis in 1938, he said of that event:

> And at this hour of the day it is no good saying
> 'Take away this cup';
> Having helped to fill it ourselves, it is only logic
> That now we should drink it up.

That is characteristically the tone of his colloquial poems, into which he packs all the paraphernalia of the modern world in a riot of imagery—buses, guns, diabetes, Picasso, museums, golf, bank-accounts, shaving, factories, films, jazz. This wide range of superficial modern reference is particularly apparent in his 'eclogues'—modern versions of the classical and Renaissance dialogues between shepherds. In these, all the apparatus and decay of modern civilisation appear even more often and more intensively than in his other work. His love of shock treatment can be seen there, too; in 'An Eclogue for Christmas', for example, which begins

> A. I meet you in an evil time.
> B.   The evil bells
>   Put out of our heads, I think, the thought of everything else.

Here all the stock associations with Christmas are meant to

be shattered at the first blow. And the poem ends with a typically agnostic statement, in which all doubt and all belief are left open and empirical:

> Goodbye to you, this day remember is Christmas, this morn
> They say, interpret it your own way, Christ is born.

Just how basic this agnosticism is in MacNeice can be seen if one turns from this poem, written in about 1934, to Canto XXV of 'Autumn Sequel', written twenty years later; the Canto ends

>   the skies are warning
> That a new sun is rising and that now,
> Take it what way you like, is really Christmas morning.

But there is also the lyrical poet—sometimes MacNeice at his best—in 'The Sunlight on the Garden', 'Cradle Song', and 'Snow'. These occasionally show the tenderness which he elsewhere effectively disguises under a mask of toughness; in this dualism perhaps we can see the Irishman (which he is by origin), as we can also see it in his talkative, disillusioned poetic character; he has written some savage but nostalgic poems about Ireland. He is one of the few contemporary poets who has managed to write satirical verse without bowing under the yoke of Pope and Dryden (the heroic couplet having strangled satire for three hundred years), and 'Bagpipe Music'—which should be read aloud, not analysed —is a good example of this.

His wry disillusionment can well be seen in little in 'Les Sylphides'. The situation is simple: a young man takes his girl to the ballet, and the romantic fantasy-world which they see on the stage moves him into his own fantasy-world, where

> there is no separation, from now on
> You will be wearing white
> Satin and a red sash
> Under the waltzing trees.

The fantasy becomes fact; the two are married. But the fact is life, and life is dull:

> So they were married—to be the more together—
> And found they were never again so much together,
> Divided by the morning tea,
> By the evening paper,
> By children and tradesmen's bills.

The situation and MacNeice's implied comment are beautifully done, with extreme suggestiveness and yet extreme economy. It is a witty poem; and perhaps when one has said all that one has said enough. But I think it is relevant to point out that the poet's viewpoint is as romantic as that of the young man in the poem, in his unquestioning belief that romantic love is as insubstantial as fantasy and that 'real life' is unremittingly dull; the disillusion is Byronic, and indeed I sometimes think of MacNeice as a sort of contemporary Byron—modified and qualified by all that has come into existence since the early nineteenth century.

One of MacNeice's most ambitious and most technically adventurous poems is 'Prayer Before Birth', which keeps an excellent balance between sentimentality and toughness. The shape of the poem itself is an expression of its theme— the slow, hesitant urging forth of the child from the womb.

The internal rhymes and the repetitive syntax make the poem incantatory, the tone becoming more and more insistent, more and more desperate, as the rhythm increases. Each section is carefully worked out, from the shunning of those creatures, real and imaginary, which terrify childhood, through prayers against outside coercion and for inner light, through forgiveness for delegated wrongdoing, through the plea to

rehearse me
In the parts I must play and the cues I must take,

to the final prayer for individuality and freedom, without which life is death: 'Otherwise kill me'. Going beyond the contemporary, and thus beyond his occasional temptations to be slick and modish, MacNeice has achieved in this poem something which is timeless, and by stretching his talents (instead of working neatly within them) he has shown that he need not merely be the poet of 'l'homme moyen sensuel' or the man in the street; though certainly his commonest gifts lie in that direction.

DAY LEWIS

The oldest of the group, Cecil Day Lewis (b. 1904), has leaned most heavily on the achievements of others. He began as a thoroughly unremarkable Georgian poet, and Georgian whimsicality and 'naturising' have been frequent stumbling-blocks in his way ever since. The first poem of his to attract attention, the long *Transitional Poem* (1929), was

C.P.—7

energetic, but—like the two long poems which succeeded it, *The Magnetic Mountain* and *From Feathers to Iron*—was too often dragged down by his adoption—sometimes astonishingly close—of some of Auden's most irritating mannerisms, such as the occasional false heartiness of lines like

> Then I'll hit the trail for that promising land;
> May catch up with Wystan and Rex my friend.

He was also, in his poetry and elsewhere, the most aggressively communist of the four, sometimes producing what can only be called versified political pamphlets—poems such as that which begins 'Why do we all, seeing a Red, feel small?'

Yet there was enormous vigour and sincerity in many of the early poems, despite the strident, aggressive tone. The sequence *From Feathers to Iron*, which follows the progress towards the birth of his child, contains some fine lyrics, ranging from the rich sensuousness of 'Do not expect again a phoenix hour' to the terse, spare poem beginning

> And since, though young, I know
> Not to expect much good,
> Our dreams from first to last
> Being treacherous underfoot.

And his contemporary imagery, though it is sometimes forced (as in such a line as 'When the charged batteries of desire . . .'), at other times has a relevance and truth, and fits easily into his impulsive and eager language; contrast this wish for his child with the uneasy juxtaposition of natural and mechanical imagery at the end of Spender's 'The Express':

Lucky, will have also
An outward grace to ease
The axles of your world
And keep the parts at peace:
Not the waste random stuff
That stops the gannet's wing;
I mean, such oil ensures
A turbine's smooth running.

Day Lewis is at his best in such personal poems as this, when his roots are in natural things and in love—either happy, lyrical love, or the nostalgic brooding of desolation; it is interesting to compare the first (especially in *From Feathers to Iron*) with the second (in such later poems as 'The Woman Alone' and 'A Failure'). The poems which move out of this individual range are generally unsatisfactory, because Day Lewis is not adept at making the broad generalisation (as Auden and MacNeice, in their different ways, are). 'You that love England', for example, is obviously meant to be didactic, and specifically revolutionary; but the imagery is either too contrived and decorative (as in the first stanza, where natural things are painfully stretched into musical analogies, instead of being organically conceived, as they are elsewhere in his straight 'nature' poetry) or too determinedly ordinary (as in the patronising reference to the week-end excursionists 'on tandem or on pillion' from the town, where one feels Day Lewis's remoteness from the lower-middle-class background he is trying to embrace in the social revolution).

In his later work, Day Lewis seems often to find inspiration in Hardy's poetry, and his diction and verse-structure show this; though the result is a Hardy softened and a little sentimentalised, without the crabbedness and angularity. The later poems, too, owe something to Meredith, and in particular to Meredith's sonnet-sequence, *Modern Love*; written in early middle age, after the break-up of his first marriage, these poems of Day Lewis's obviously draw on material close to Meredith's own experience. The question is, how does one judge a twentieth century poet who, after helping achieve the poetic revolution of our time, reacts in his prime by writing work which is a pastiche—very competent pastiche—of two eminent Victorian poets? Such a poem as 'The Unwanted', for example, is Hardy with all the edges knocked off. There is no doubt that Day Lewis has a liking for pastiche, as one can see if one turns to Part Five of *An Italian Visit* (1953), which is a sequence of poems 'after' or 'in the manner of' five well-known poets; a deliberate poetic exercise, and the Hardy, the Yeats and the Auden are astonishing *tours de forces*. But can he continue as an independent poet in this way? Obviously not, and one can only hope that one day he will manage either to return to the manner in which his most successful work has been done, or else strike out into new territory.

CHAPTER EIGHT

Dylan Thomas

(1914–1953)

and George Barker

(b. 1913)

Dylan Thomas died, at the age of 39, in November 1953. In the days and months that followed, there was a show of public mourning and legend-building unequalled, as far as any literary figure has been concerned, in our time. The *News Chronicle* gave the event a large headline: 'The poet they called a dangerous cherub'. The *Daily Mail* more recently published a series of five articles on 'The Most Fantastic Character of Our Time'. Even *The Times*, with its great reputation for seriousness and restraint, gave him an obituary three times as long as usual. Papers and magazines were full of reminiscences by people 'who knew Dylan'; it was significant that they all seemed to know him by his first name. And Dame Edith Sitwell, with her gift for the dramatic and the rhetorical, sent a telegram from Hollywood to Laugharne, where Thomas was buried: 'To the greatest poet of the younger generation lying in his grave I send devotion undying as his poetry is deathless.'

The reasons for the popular adulation were mainly non-literary. Dylan Thomas, as a personality, was exactly what the public *likes* a poet to be—drunken, witty, bold, exuberant, careless in his habits, a spendthrift, Rabelaisian in his speech. As a reader of poetry at public recitals and on the radio, he had great and individual gifts; and his one appearance on television, when he read one of his own stories, must alone have brought him a far wider and more appreciative audience than a modern poet can generally expect. His death, brought on because of excessive drinking and a haphazard daily life, seemed to some people to be either a kind of unconscious suicide (the poet bowing before the forces of philistinism) or else collective murder (materialistic society crushing an individual it could not absorb).

I consider both views to be absurd and hysterical, and as unpleasant as the embarrassing reminiscences I mentioned above. The whole 'Dylan legend' is in danger of smothering any real consideration of his poetry. Even now, some of the younger critics are beginning to say that Thomas was over-rated, that really he was a minor poet. This, I think, is to swing too far in the opposite direction. What one has to do is to look fairly and squarely at the poems themselves, seeing them without sentimental distortion or sour critical prejudice, insofar as one can. After all, there is a reasonable body of work to consider; Thomas—for all the maudlin references to his youth—was 39 when he died; almost exactly the same age as Wyatt, Herbert and Byron, and considerably older than Marlowe, Keats and Shelley. And Thomas's *Collected Poems*, published about a year before his death, can be looked at as a whole, and not simply as the unfinished foundations of a building.

Thomas's first book, *Eighteen Poems*, was published when he was just twenty, in 1934. Auden's first book of poems had appeared four years before; Auden, Spender and Day Lewis were considered to be the best representative young poets. On this world of 'social relevance' and 'the objective cor-relative' and 'the poet as reporter', *Eighteen Poems* made a deep impression. Here was poetry which was full of verbal intoxication and verbal compulsion; a personal, introvert, obsessive poetry. The mind which created them seemed to be fixed on a small range of themes and to be restricted to a small range of techniques, yet the general effect was of a fascinatingly fluent and inventive genius. The two themes are sex and death, and the two are often identified as the same thing; the speaker or *persona* of the poems is frequently a child in the womb, or similar protomorphic being:

> Before I knocked and flesh let enter,
> With liquid hands tapped on the womb,
> I who was shapeless as the water
> That shaped the Jordan near my home
> Was brother to Mnetha's daughter
> And sister to the fathering worm.
>
> I who was deaf to spring and summer,
> Who knew not sun nor moon by name,
> Felt thud beneath my flesh's armour,
> As yet was in a molten form,
> The leaden stars, the rainy hammer
> Swung by my father from his dome.

These are stanzas from a poem which is a re-created 'memory' of life in the womb by a myth-figure who, in the last few lines, is seen as identified with Christ himself:

> You who bow down at cross and altar,
> Remember me and pity Him
> Who took my flesh and bone for armour
> And doublecrossed my mother's womb.

'Doublecrossed' should be taken as a pun—A) the protagonist in the poem is seen as literally crossing the womb twice, first as his own self-begetter and then as the child itself (Christ is both the Son of God and God himself); B) the womb is 'doublecrossed' (tricked or cheated) because it is made to bring forth beings who die.

Thomas's early poems begin with the assumption or insistence that we start to die from the moment we are born —even, indeed, from the time we are conceived. And this continual process of dying links us with everything else in the world: the death of a flower comes under the same edict and force as our own death, because the powers of destruction are united. This is a theme with which he deals in one of his best-known early poems, of which the following is the first stanza:

> The force that through the green fuse drives the flower
> Drives my green age; that blasts the roots of trees
> Is my destroyer.
> And I am dumb to tell the crooked rose
> My youth is bent by the same wintry fever.

These poems were original and strange when they first appeared, and some of them—perhaps half a dozen—must be put among Thomas's best work. They were not, however, the poems of a complete naif or primitive, as some critics at one time assumed; Thomas, after all, was the son of an English master at Swansea Grammar School, and he himself attended that school until he was sixteen. He was widely read, despite all the tales about his taste for cowboy stories and children's comics. Certainly he must have begun to read the poems of Hopkins and the prose of James Joyce in his adolescence; the stylistic traces of these two writers can be found in a great deal of his work. Yet temperamentally he was remote from them, having neither the Christian discipline of Hopkins nor the eccentric pedantry of Joyce. As Karl Shapiro, the American poet, has written:

> The language of Thomas is very close to that of Hopkins, not only in obvious ways, but in its very method. Hopkins, however, arrived at his method philosophically, abstractly, as well as through temperament and the twist of his personality. Thomas, with no equipment for theorizing about the forms of nature, sought the 'forms' that Hopkins did.

The obscurity of Dylan Thomas is not, therefore based on the same reasons as that of Hopkins; the difficulties are always verbal, never intellectual. This can become dangerous, and one does sometimes have the feeling that Thomas was being (in the phrase used by reactionary critics of any modern poetry) 'wilfully obscure'.

Thomas's range and manner seemed hardly to grow in his second book, *Twenty-Five Poems*, though in that volume there were two pieces which stood out as possible extensions beyond his sex-death obsession: 'The hand that signed the paper' and 'And Death shall have no dominion'. The first is almost a metaphysical conceit on the subject of power, and someone has pointed out that the last two lines remind one of Herbert or some other seventeenth century poet:

> A hand rules pity as a hand rules heaven;
> Hands have no tears to flow.

The second poem, though it is concerned with his abiding theme of death, is different because of its superb arrogance, its repudiation of destruction and nullity, which one can compare with Donne's sonnet 'Death, be not proud'. The rhetoric is unloosed, and the poem seems to exist in a harsh clear world, not the dark secret world of the other death-poems.

It was in his third book, *The Map of Love*, that Thomas included (in his own words)

> the only poem I ever wrote directly about the life and death of one particular human being I knew—and not about the very many lives and deaths, whether seen, as in my first poems, in the tumultuous world of my own being or, as in the later poems, in war, grief, and the great holes and corners of universal love.

This is 'After the Funeral' (sometimes known by its sub-title, 'In Memory of Ann Jones'). It is an elegy for the old aunt with whom Thomas used to spend many of his holidays in the depths of rural Wales when he was a child. Ann Jones appears in one of the stories ('The Peaches') in Thomas's book of semi-autobiographical pieces, *Portrait of the Artist as a Young Dog*, where she is described as 'a little, brown-skinned, toothless, hunchbacked woman with a cracked, sing-song voice'. Not only is Ann (or Annie, as she is called in the story) described, but also the room in her cottage which, with its ferns and stuffed fox, is the setting of the poem. This poem, therefore, has a closely particularised relation to Thomas's personal life—and this is rare in his poetry.

'After the Funeral' can be divided into three parts—the funeral and funeral-feast; the bard's disclaimer; and the celebration or 'keen' over Ann's memory. These divisions are somewhat confused, mainly because of Thomas's anarchic punctuation. (I often have the feeling that this is a central trouble in many of Thomas's poems, and I have no hesitation in revising the punctuation when it helps the sense.) The poem begins with an impressionistic picture of the funeral, with its donkey-like braying over the dead body, its ostentatious sorrow and ritualistic mourning; against this is set the

> muffle-toed tap
> Tap happily of one peg in the thick
> Grave's foot

as the earth is thrown back on to the coffin. The noise of the spade shakes the poet back to his memories of Ann when he was a child, and he 'slits his throat' in the gesture children use when they make a promise; his promise is that he will never forget her. He is too moved to weep; he 'sheds dry leaves' whereas the mourners are openly snivelling into their sleeves, wiping the tears away. He stands alone in the room he remembers from his childhood, 'a room with a stuffed fox and a stale fern', and remembers also Ann's kindness, which was like a hidden fountain, nourishing all who came into contact with her in the 'parched worlds of Wales'. (The poem is Celtic in its setting and its bardic spirit.) Then the poet considers that such an image is too fulsome and wordy to please her spirit; she does not need a druid or bardic priest to pronounce a histrionic oration over her. Instead, he calls on nature to celebrate her love and her 'bent spirit'; the funeral is thus transferred in the poet's mind to the natural world, where her own natural virtue is the bell which calls the people to church, where the church itself is made by the trees bowing down (both in homage and to make an arch above her—in 'the ferned and foxy woods', which give a link with the dead fox and fern in the house) and where the cross is formed by four birds flying in the sky above. Now that she is dead, she goes through a creative metamorphosis in his mind; the humble flesh becomes a huge statue in memory of her, and though he knows that her real hands, voice and mind are now still, her strong little face twisted from the pain in which she died, she has become a monument, 'seventy years of stone'. Let these monuments of her body and spirit inspire him, he says, so that even the dead fox will be reborn and the dead fern create new life.

The method of 'After the Funeral' is one of contradiction and opposition, and in this connection it is useful to quote one of Thomas's few statements on his own poetry:

> a poem by myself needs a host of images, because its centre is a host of images. I make one image—though 'make' is not the word; I let, perhaps, an image be 'made' emotionally in me and then apply to it what intellectual and critical forces I possess; let it breed another, let that image contradict the first; make of the third image, bred out of the other two together, a fourth contradictory image, and let them all, within my imposed formal limits, conflict . . . The life in any poem of mine cannot move concentrically round a central image, the life must come out of the centre; an image must be born and die in another; and any sequence of my image must be a sequence of creations, recreations, destructions, contradictions . . .

The main images on which this poem turns are A) the fox and the fern, and B) the real Ann and the Ann whom the poet creates in his mind, 'a monstrous image blindly magnified out of praise'. These images are expanded, re-created and tied. The fox and the fern are objects in the stuffy, dead room of the dead woman—symbols, in fact, of that stuffiness and deadness. The word 'stuffed' as applied to the fox is obviously meant to carry the associations of its semi-homonym 'stuffy'; and the funeral feast becomes 'the feast of tear-stuffed time'—the neighbours' and relatives' mourning is full of tears just as the fox (like the old woman) is full of age. The dead woman is juxtaposed with the dead fox which was her lifetime companion. Later, however, the fox and fern are transferred to their natural habitat, the wood which becomes (in the poet's mind) Ann's chapel. And in the end both are seen as representing the dead which might be brought to life by Ann's love.

The real Ann is a simple countrywoman, worn out by hard work, hunchbacked, wizened, kind; set against her is the monument which the 'bard' (Thomas himself) carves for her—the contrast between 'her flesh was meek as milk' and 'this skyward statue', between 'her scrubbed and sour humble hands' and 'These cloud-sopped, marble hands'. The real woman is not simply *made* by the poet into a monument: within the poem, she *grows* to that stature.

I have concentrated on 'After the Funeral' because it makes a more coherent (and hence more moving) impression than many of Thomas's other poems, and because it illustrates so well his general method. His last book of poems (before his collected volume), *Deaths and Entrances*, includes a number which deal with 'war, grief, and the great holes and corners of universal love', poems such as 'A Refusal to Mourn the Death, by Fire, of a Child in London', 'Ceremony after a Fire Raid', and 'Dawn Raid'. But there are also several which draw on his nostalgia for childhood, having a link with 'After the Funeral': these are 'The Hunchback in the Park', 'Poem in October', 'Poem on his birthday' and 'Fern Hill'. In these poems, as in Traherne and Wordsworth, childhood is seen as a state of absolute innocence and grace from which man declines through the years. The child is involved in the process of time, and hence of death, though he does not know it then:

> And nothing I cared, at my sky blue trades, that time allows
> In all his tuneful turning so few and such morning songs
>   Before the children green and golden
>   Follow him out of grace . . .
> Oh as I was young and easy in the mercy of his means,
>   Time held me green and dying
>   Though I sang in my chains like the sea.

Yet there are moments in maturity when that childhood suddenly becomes real again; in particular, birthdays remind the man of the child he once was; and both 'Poem in October' and 'Poem on his birthday' turn on this idea—the first at the age of thirty and the second at thirty-five. Life moves towards death, and so in 'Poem in October'

> It was my thirtieth year *to heaven*
> Woke to my hearing . . .

It is a more wistful, less savage, development of the theme of so many of his earlier poems:

> In the groin of the natural doorway I crouched like a tailor
> Sewing a shroud for a journey
> By the light of the meat-eating sun.

The later poems have, in their movement and language, an air of careless improvisation which was probably deliberate; they lack the tautness and strong compulsive rhythms of *Eighteen Poems* and *Twenty-Five Poems*, and are in fact much closer in technique to his prose in *Portrait of the Artist* and in his unfinished novel, *Adventures in the Skin Trade*. In 'Fern

Hill', for example, the word 'lovely' is used twice in three lines—a colourless word when compared with the strong, and even eccentric, adjectives which are characteristic of the earlier Thomas:

> All the sun long it was running, it was lovely, the hay
> Fields high as the house, the tunes from the chimneys, it was air
> And playing, lovely and watery . . .

It can be explained as an attempt to give the air of unconsidered and artless delight which a child experiences; but such slackness of tension is dangerous in a poet who leads one to savour words rather than ideas. It seems to me that as his range increased, his technique deteriorated.

It would be wrong to end on this note. Reading through the *Collected Poems*, one is convinced that, despite faults of apparent carelessness, bombast and even faking, Dylan Thomas was a major poet. In the future, he will probably be seen as a much less 'important' poet than Yeats, Eliot and Auden (in the sense that little can be learned from him; what influence he has had on other poets has been almost wholly bad); yet he wrote at least a dozen poems which I think the future will put in the best canon of English poetry. And that is more important than any legends or any criticism.

GEORGE BARKER

George Barker, a year older than Thomas, published his first book in 1933; he was thus, like Thomas, an early developer. What these early poems chiefly showed was great verbal ferment and a pessimism which, at that time, seemed to have little real object. In such a poem as 'On First Hearing Beethoven', the words seem literally to drown the sense:

> Whose absolute dumbness circumscribed by sound
> Dumbfounds and profoundly confounds the boundary
> Of my sense, I hear, in dense silence founded
> By supernal sound, the immense harmonic like mountains
> Intensely imbedded in man in agony bound and drowned.

This excessive wordiness has continued to be a blot on Barker's work, sometimes transcended when he has had a unifying theme, sometimes not. In 1934 he wrote, in answer to a question about his poetic method: 'I feel myself very powerfully conscious of the purely verbal origin of a poem; that the impulse is "spontaneous" I suspect, but cannot verify.' Words are therefore the begetters of other words, and the critical intelligence is often neglected. Thus one gets a certain amount of rhetorical excitement, but not much of a central thread of sense.

Barker is perfectly well aware of this common-sensical criticism, but he rejects it with gusto; he has written

> . . . it is absolutely essential for the poet to bite off more than he can chew. By this method he may enlarge the human appetite for all things. But if he bites off no more than he can masticate, he proves little more than we already know: he is merely a man having a meal . . . Personally I have never been on the side of the angelic perfectionists. I believe that perfect poetry is no more possible than perfect people. And I believe that if you have got to make mistakes you might as well make great mistakes, because these will at least show other people what not to do . . . When Shakespeare put down the pen and died he had committed a hundred and one mistakes of excess and commission, but he had also discovered the English language.

Having read this, we at least know where we are with Barker; it is then possible to discover why he is very much worth reading, and then to deplore the fact that he is much less well-known than he should be. Too often he has been regarded as a rather less important Dylan Thomas, and the reaction which is obscuring Thomas's work is obscuring Barker's too.

The first thing to notice is that Barker is a religious poet; religious not in the sense that Hopkins was, but like Baudelaire. A critic has said that his theme is thus: 'Because we live, we live in error.' But that is to simplify too much; there is particular guilt at particular error—the fact that man is a sexual animal. In his poetic novel *The Dead Seagull*, Barker quotes the following passage by Cardinal Newman:

> . . . *if* there be a God, *since* there is a God, the human race is implicated in some terrible aboriginal calamity. It is out of joint with the purposes of its Creator. This is a fact as true as the fact of its existence, and thus the doctrine of what is theologically called original sin becomes to me almost as certain as that the world exists, and as the existence of God.

And Barker adds:

> . . . I have discovered the nature and name of the mystery he terms 'some terrible aboriginal calamity', the calamity in which we necessarily labour . . . It is love. Yes, Love is the terrible aboriginal calamity.

Finally (again, from *The Dead Seagull*):

> It is love that destroys us with the killer of sex. Sex without love is utterly incapable of sin; this is the coupling of beasts in a moral void. Love without sex is the great prince in prison.

C.P.—8

All human suffering, he implies, comes from the egotism or abuses or perversions of love; violence, whether in war or in personal relationships, is a product of this. Yet he sees the process as inevitable; we must accept and tame it. In man's damnation, suffering at least is real:

> I know only that the heart
> Doubting every real thing else
> Does not doubt the voice that tells
> Us that we suffer. The hard part
> At the dead centre of the soul
> Is an age of frozen grief
> No vernal equinox of relief
> Can mitigate, and no love console.

Barker's youthful pessimism thus found a proper object— proper whether we agree with it or not. Within the context of his religious feeling of guilt, his poems become like lurid fragments from the confessional in a Roman Catholic church (Barker himself was born and brought up as a Roman Catholic, and still considers himself one). If, as Cyril Connolly has said, a poet today should be judged by 'the resonance of his solitude and the quality of his despair', then Barker is an important poet; and the religio-moral problems which drive him to this solitude and despair are indeed important.

A fair example of his concerns, his faults and his triumphs, is *The True Confession of George Barker*, a long poem first published in pamphlet form (it was rejected by Fabers, his usual publishers, because of its occasional obscenity), a spiritual autobiography. It contains a mixture of the most turgid and childish filth together with passages which are among the finest written in this century. As Kenneth Allott has said of Barker in general:

The truth, as I see it, is that few poets can have written so well and so badly inside the covers of one volume, sometimes inside a single poem.

This can be seen in both the Barker poems which Allott includes in his anthology. The first, 'Battersea Park', is a meditation on the idea that the world is a sorrowful place, because its beauties remind us that it is transient. It is also, perhaps, analogous to Shelley's line from 'To a Skylark',

Our sweetest songs are those that tell of saddest thought.

The meditation begins at a particular season and in a particular place: November, and in Battersea Park by the Thames in London. The fog and his sorrow at his own perpetual disillusionment are linked seasonally; the dreams and aspirations which sprang up in him in April and 'burned so bright' in August are now scattered. The 'bare gardens' through which he walks are symbols of the world which so cruelly 'revives desire to live once more'. Then his sorrow appears to him personified—and it is at this point that the poem takes a false step; Sorrow is seen with a levity which is quite out of keeping with the rest of the meditation. This has nothing to do with Auden's 'lightness of tone'; it is simply a lack of sureness, a desire to make an effect for its own sake. Yet— typically—Barker quickly regains control, and leads us into the very fine sixth stanza:

> And he went on, singing a gay tune.
> And now I know that the sorrow is this,
> Not that the world a space of sorrow is
> But that it's glad. O so gay a grief!
> How can I ever be at home here
> Where Sorrow sings of Joy in my ear?

At this point the poem might well have ended, but Barker, with his sometimes fatal fluency, persists with a development of these lines, so that the final effect is rather dissipated. It is the romantic's danger of never knowing when to stop (a similar fault disfigures some of Dylan Thomas's long poems, such as 'The Ballad of the Long-Legged Bait' and 'In Country Sleep'). Yet the lack of unifying power is, in my opinion, greatly compensated for by the incidental excitements and beauties.

In the second poem, 'To My Mother', this fault—which can perhaps be called lack of taste—disfigures only the final line. Barker has written many sonnets, of which this is one, but on the whole one feels that the form does not suit him; he is too turbulent and too careless to cage himself so narrowly. Yet here the characteristics of his mother, described with a sort of loving exaggeration, unify the poem. He is far away from her (the poem was written sometime between 1939 and 1943, when Barker was in Japan and America), and his mind re-creates her picture—fat, her huge body shaken with laughter as by an earthquake, massive in her presence and her appetites, yet also gentle to all creatures. Massively imperturbable, the dangers of war cannot shake her; she is 'like a mountain / Whom only faith can move'. All this is very well said, with an appealing mixture of the gently tender and the robustly comic. Yet there is no resolution:

> and so I send
> O all my faith and all my love to tell her
> That she will move from mourning into morning.

Obviously words are trying to do here what sentiment cannot; there is a mere verbal compulsion about the link between 'mourning' and 'morning', and there is nothing in the rest of the poem which has decently led us to this conclusion.

Why then read George Barker, if his faults are so glaring? Consider his own remarks on perfectionism, which I quoted earlier; and then consider this epigram by Roy Campbell (it is 'On Some South African Novelists', but it fits the case perfectly well):

> You praise the firm restraint with which they write—
> I'm with you there, of course:
> They use the snaffle and the curb all right,
> But where's the bloody horse?

Barker often neglects 'the snaffle and the curb', but he *has* 'the bloody horse'. The fire, the energy, the calculated violence and the deep moral passion make him remarkable. He cannot adequately be criticised (as I have shown in this chapter), because the critic feels that disclaimers and qualifying judgments must continually be made, and these tend to get in the way of the positive achievements.

CHAPTER NINE

Some other poets of the 1930s and 1940s

There are sixty-one poets represented in Allott's *Contemporary Verse*; and since the present book deals with only thirteen of these in detail (plus Hopkins, whom Allott excluded), it may be wondered which of the other fifty are worth notice. They cannot, on the whole, be dealt with satisfactorily by dividing them into 'groups' and 'trends' because, if such divisions have any value at all, it is generally only well after the event that they can be usefully applied. I propose to deal individually with about a dozen of them who came into some prominence between about 1930 and 1945.

The one man in this chapter who has qualities which sometimes make him seem a major poet is Roy Campbell (1901–1957). His poetic personality was vigorous, masculine and prolific; and one can say of his lack of smoothness and restraint, as Dryden said of John Oldham,

> But Satyr needs not those, and Wit will shine
> Through the harsh cadence of a rugged line.
> A noble Error, and but seldom made,
> When Poets are by too much force betray'd.

Not that he lacked in technical inventiveness, and even virtuosity. His rollicking metres are sometimes tied to rhymes so ingenious that they seem to have come from a Rhyming

Dictionary (a book, by the way, not to be despised, but unusual rhymes in English too often sound merely comic; thus
'chirrup' and 'syrup', 'engines' and 'vengeance', in 'Poets in
Africa'). The blurb on the back of his *Collected Poems* says
that he 'very early acquired a passionate love for literature
and adventure that has never left him'; the trouble is that one
sometimes wonders whether he always knew which was
which. Born in South Africa, where he raged against the
philistinism and provincialism of the country, he became
something of a deliberate philistine himself when he came to
England, and raged equally fiercely against what he considered
to be the effeminacy and in-bred quality of English literary
life. As a Roman Catholic and almost Yeatsian believer in
'nobility' and 'aristocracy', he was one of the few English
intellectuals to support Franco's cause during the Spanish
Civil War, and the only one actually to fight for the 'Loyal-
ists' (i.e. Fascists). 'The Georgiad', a satire on English literary
personalities of the early 1930s, made him one set of enemies,
and such lyrics as 'Hot Rifles' and 'Christ in Uniform'—
seeing the war in Spain as a holy crusade against the infidel—
made him another. Yet if one can make the difficult Cole-
ridgean 'suspension of disbelief', one can see energy and
virtue even in his most savage and idiosyncratic poems. As
a satirist, he advanced no further than Dryden, Pope and
Byron, yet he is the only poet of the present age who worked
effectively in the forms these poets perfected. And as a writer
of lyrics, he was full of verbal invention and zest, especially
when he could spread himself, in such an extended lyric as
'The Palm'. What prevented him from being more important and successful is that he was far too often too determinedly exuberant, so that (like Swinburne) his force
becomes purely verbal, his wild rhymes and diction rush on
and on, and eventually the reader becomes tired, wondering—

the most damning thing of all—when the poem is going to stop.

Kathleen Raine and Anne Ridler are two women whose poetry shows (in contradiction to remarks frequently made by male critics) that mere sensibility is not what one should necessarily expect from feminine verse. Kathleen Raine (b. 1909) has been the more highly praised of the two, perhaps because she is more obviously adventurous, yet I do not feel that her more unconventional work is her most successful; steeped in Blake, in whose poetry she takes a scholarly as well as a poetic interest, her transparent use of symbolism—by which merely to name is to symbolise—is as unsatisfactory as Blake's in the *Prophetic Books*. Such poems may sometimes have light, but they never have substance; they are caught by the eye, but vanish if one looks at them closely. This may be my personal blindness; G. S. Fraser quotes the following poem and praises it highly, but to me it is no more than an incantatory pattern of words: it is called 'The World':

> It burns in the void,
> Nothing upholds it.
> Still it travels.
>
> Travelling the void
> Upheld by burning
> Nothing is still.
>
> Burning it travels.
> The void upholds it.
> Still it is nothing.
>
> Nothing it travels
> A burning void
> Upheld by stillness.

If you like that, you will like Kathleen Raine's work; if
not, not. This, and the sort of breathless pantheism one finds
in 'Passion', seem to me to carry speculation beyond the
point to which poetry can carry it. Some of her slighter and
more purely lyrical pieces are much better, I think; and her
song, 'The Spring' shows, among other things, that some of
the best 'personal' lyrics (such as those of the Elizabethans)
are, strangely enough, impersonal.

Anne Ridler (b. 1912) is, in a sense, a much more limited
poet, but perhaps that is her strength. In her quiet celebration
of domestic and religious subjects, she is never strained, yet on
the other hand she is never slight or trivial. Her love for her
family and her love of God are complementary, so that the
most ordinary personal events—the birth of a child, a tem-
porary parting, a holiday—become somehow sacramental.
What one is aware of more than anything else in her
poetry is the essential decency of ordinary human relationships, and that—after so much powerful and compelling work
which implies the contrary—is refreshing. Take, for example,
the last stanza of 'At Parting':

> We cannot quite cast out lack and pain.
> Let him remain—what he may devour
> We can well spare:
> He never can tap this, the true vein.
> I have no words to tell you what you were,
> But when you are sad, think, Heaven could give no more.

No individual part of that is remarkable; the idea of absence
'devouring', the idea of tapping a mineral-vein, the generally
unfigurative language—each is, by itself, commonplace; but
together, knitted by great purity of diction and great colloquial subtlety of rhythm, each helps to build a satisfying
and moving whole. This investing of the commonplace with

distinction can appear even in individual passages, which surprise one not with their novelty but with their power of expressing truths unaffectedly and economically. Thus, she says of a child in the womb:

> And when our baby stirs and struggles to be born
> It compels humility: what we began
> Is now its own.

Her powers of directness and restraint, together with her lyrical gift, are most impressive in her long poem, 'A Matter of Life and Death', a meditation on birth and childhood. And her religious poetry is as close in spirit to Herbert and Traherne as anything written in the present century, without being in any way imitative.

Another poet who sometimes reminds one of seventeenth century writers is F. T. Prince (b. 1912). At other times, his work seems like a skilful translation from some foreign language; the words seem just slightly twisted out of the norm, so that one is oddly disturbed and delighted. Some lines from 'False Bay' will show what I mean:

> She I love leaves me and I leave my friends
> In the dusky capital where I spent two years
> In the cultivation of divinity.
> Sitting beside my window above the sea
> In this unvisited land I feel once more
> How little ingenious I am . . .

This reminds me of something I cannot quite put my finger on—a translation from the Greek Anthology, or a memory of Ovid at Tomi. 'The cultivation of divinity', 'this unvisited land' and 'how little ingenious I am' are unusually fastidious phrases; and fastidiousness, of tone and diction, is a distinctive feature of Prince's work. In his love poems, such as 'The Inn', 'The Dice', 'The Diamond', this gives him the appearance of being a smoother Donne. This, for example, from the beginning of 'The Inn':

> February is the shortest month and good
> For this too, that we shall be one
> With the campaigning season and, that done,
> If I go where I would not by the way
> I would not, on my journey I may say
> That as it was, it will be, and I should
> Come back the way I would to where I would.

No one, since Eliot's earlier poems, has been able to use Donne's methods as successfully as this; the danger is that it trembles on the edge of being pastiche. In his poems of broader gesture, such as 'Soldiers Bathing', he is more purely himself, though his structure, which is so neat in the shorter poems, tends to become sprawling when he attempts bigger things. This criticism, however, cannot be made of 'Soldiers Bathing' itself, which seems to me to be one of the major poems of our time; indeed, there is no doubt that it overshadows everything else Prince has written. Taking as its starting point the sight of a group of soldiers bathing in the sea during a lull in fighting during the Second World War, it moves on to link the scene with a Michelangelo drawing of Florentine soldiers, also bathing, surprised by the enemy; the fragility and purity of the naked bodies about to be slaughtered reminds him

> that rage, that bitterness, those blows,
> That hatred of the slain, what could it be
> But indirectly or brutally a commentary

On the Crucifixion for the picture burns
With indignation and pity and despair and love by turns
Because it is the obverse of the scene
Where Christ hangs murdered, stripped, upon the Cross: I mean,
That is the explanation of its rage.

Violence and peace, thrown together, are at the very heart of the Christian story, and in this scene they have the clarity of a parable.

The quantity of Henry Reed's (b. 1914) work, like that of Prince, is small, and his best work may be that which is least overtly serious; I mean his sequence of three poems called 'Lessons of the War'. These are ironical meditations on three elements of a modern soldier's basic training—the categorical naming of the component parts of a rifle, the methodical ability to judge a distance correctly, and combat without weapons. 'Naming of Parts' contrasts the rifle-mechanism (lower sling swivel, safety-catch, bolt, breech, point of balance), and all its implications of organised destruction, with the natural progress of the Spring—blossoming bushes, flowers, bees. 'Easing the spring', for example is the technical name for the action of clearing a rifle-breech of ammunition or spent cartridges, but can also be taken as a whimsical term for the action of the bees as they burrow mindlessly into the flowers, impelled by the season. 'Point of balance' is a similar pun. 'Judging Distances', again, contrasts the natural scene with the precise, dry terms in which it must be described militarily. Everything must be reduced to its bare essentials; there is no room for emotion, or even for certainty ('You must never be over-sure'). And Reed deliberately juxtaposes an exaggeratedly romantic description of the lovers in the field with the correct military description:

> Which is, perhaps, only to say
> That there is a row of houses to the left of arc,
> And that under some poplars a pair of what appear to be humans
> Appear to be loving.

These are poems not only of ironical wit but also of direct good humour; the 'official' military voice in all of them is broadly and comically drawn:

> You must say, when reporting:
> At five o'clock in the central sector is a dozen
> Of what appear to be animals; whatever you do,
> Don't call the bleeders *sheep*.

Reed's other poems are much less outstanding and, because he has published little new verse since 1946, it seems that his reputation will have to survive on the slim but distinctive evidence of 'Lessons of the War'.

Lawrence Durrell (b. 1914) is one of several poets of this period who have drawn a great deal of their poetic nourishment from their knowledge, and love, of the Mediterranean. Yet he is not merely 'a poet of place' (a type which I find very unsatisfying), and such a poem as 'A Ballad of the Good Lord Nelson' shows that he can handle rowdy comedy as well as Auden ever did in 'Songs and Musical Pieces'. In 'Alexandria', there is no finical regard or close description of the town, yet it is also quite definitely *there*:

> And then turning where the last pale
> Lighthouse, like a Samson blinded, stands
> And turns its huge charred orbit on the sands
> I think of you . . .

And his complex but clear syntactical construction and long

rhythmical breath are apparent in the last stanza of the same
poem:

> So we, learning to suffer and not condemn
> Can only wish you this great pure wind
> Condemned by Greece, and turning like a helm
> Inland where it smokes the fires of men,
> Spins weathercocks on farms or catches
> The lovers at their quarrel in the sheets;
> Or like a walker in the darkness might,
> Knocks and disturbs the artist at his papers
> Up there alone, upon the alps of night.

He is a sensuous poet, remote both from Auden's 'clinical',
clipped quality and the verbal intoxication of Dylan Thomas,
and an elegant one, using technical tricks which succeed
because he is sophisticated enough to know just how far he
can go:

> Wrap your sulky beauty up,
> From sea-fever, from winterfall,
> Out of the swing of the
> Swing of the sea.

Roy Fuller (b. 1912) has learned from Auden the knack of
combining lightness of tone with seriousness of purpose, and
of making broad generalisations in concrete phrases. When,
in the early 1940s, he began to publish, the socially-conscious
poetry of Auden, MacNeice and the others was already going
out of the fashion, but Fuller's theoretical or idealistic Marxism could not allow him to ignore a view of man as a social
animal, rather than as an introspective word-fancier, as the
proper centre of poetry. Sometimes his manner is too close to
Auden (as in 'Ibsen', where he takes the sort of subject with
which the 1930s Auden would have dealt, and writes about

it in an Audenesque way), and he has faults of slickness and dryness. But he is always, above all, intelligent, and he likes to go straight to the heart of the problem, in straightforward colloquial terms. Here are the opening passages from three poems:

> Reading the shorthand on a barber's sheet
> In a warm and chromium basement in Cannon Street
> I discovered again the message of the city,
> That without power there is no place for pity . . .

> After a night of insomnia I read
> In the morning paper of the death of Gide,
> Who by allowing smaller men to share
> Such nights made theirs the less to bear,
> Even to answer to creative need . . .

> On the aeroplane from Nice I lost my pen,
> That instrument of poetry and affairs.
> Nor do I miss the coarser symbolism
> The minor drama so naively bares . .

Notice that the point from which he starts, here and in many of his poems, is himself; the trivial personal event, often deliberately trivially described, which acts as a lever into the general application of what he has to say. This offhand, nonchalant air can be called a mannerism, but it makes one take notice: 'Here,' Fuller seems to say, 'is something perfectly ordinary which happened to me, as it could, of course, to you . . .' and this is done without any air of condescension. The premises on which he bases his work—pessimism and distrust—are negative, but his wit and balance prevent the poems themselves from being gloomy.

Surrealism, the anti-rational literary and artistic movement which began in France and Central Europe during the late 1920s, never became really at home in England, except, perhaps, in some of Paul Nash's painting—and in the early work of David Gascoyne (b. 1916). Gascoyne was at one time called 'the only whole-hearted English Surrealist', and as a very young man he did a good deal to publicise the movement, with an exposition of the subject, a number of translations from such French Surrealists as Eluard, and his own poetry. Some of these Gascoyne poems were included in the first edition of *The Faber Book of Modern Verse*, but there is no doubt that Gascoyne would no longer be willing to be judged by them. Yet I question how truly Surrealist, how completely free of the critical censor in his own mind, Gascoyne ever was. A stanza like the following, published when he was sixteen, is—though it does not make much sense—an organised piece of writing:

> The cold renunciatory beauty of those who would die
> to hide their love from scornful fingers of the drab
> is not that which glistens like wing or leaf in eyes
> of erotic statues standing breast to chest
> on high and open mountainside.

By the time he was twenty-two, Gascoyne had almost emerged from whatever allegiance he felt for Surrealism; but his astonishingly early start, his absorption in words for their own sake, may have been a necessary preliminary to his later, ruthlessly purified work. He began to write a sequence of religious poems, called 'Miserere', all of which are concerned with the terrible spiritual desolation of those who are banished—and know that they are banished—from the sight of God. A quotation from Gascoyne's prose is relevant here: 'Man cannot endure for long the constant imminence of the aimless Void which is concomitant with denial of the Spirit.'

> Here am I now cast down
> Beneath the black glare of a netherworld's
> Dead suns, dust in my mouth, among
> Dun tiers no tears refresh: am cast
> Down by a lofty hand . . .

But even when he is allowed a vision of God, he is aware chiefly of suffering and grief:

> The Mother, whose dead Son's dear head
> Weighs like a precious blood-incrusted stone
> On her unfathomable breast . . .

Derek Stanford comments on these lines: 'Not only are we given the visual appearance of the crucified Christ, but the worth and significance of his death and its rare moral value are suggested by the image of the jewel'. This intense, nervous imagery is equally clear, outside a religious context, in 'A Wartime Dawn', where every sense seems strained with apprehension. Someone has described Gascoyne's poetry as being like the journal of a sensitive invalid, and it is precisely that fine-drawn quality which is so well recorded in the poem: every sense is alert:

> Nearest within the window's sight, ash-pale
> Against a cinder coloured wall, the white
> Pearblossom hovers like a stare . . .
> A pang of poignant odour from the earth, an unheard sigh
> Pregnant with sap's sweet tang and raw soil's fine
> Aroma, smell of stone, and acrid breath
> Of gravel puddles . . .

C.P.—9

Gascoyne is, to make a bad pun, a mystic without a *mystique*; what he is most aware of is disbelief and negation, and his senses are stretched to breaking point to achieve something more positive. Yet neither in the real world nor the ideal world can he find it:

> The way to Life is through the entrance into Night:
> The recognition of the Night wherein each man
> Must have at first existence . . .

Finally, I must briefly mention some of the poets whose apparent promise was cut off by their death in the Second World War: Alun Lewis, Sidney Keyes, Keith Douglas and Drummond Allison. Lewis (1915–1944), as Allott suggests, might have developed rather as a prose-writer than as a poet if he had lived, and his poems are often too loaded with atmospheric descriptiveness to be more than static, despite the fact that he obviously (in prose) had narrative power. 'The Mahratta Ghats' begins well, with an evocative picture of India, but the attempt to force it to a concluding moral is a failure. Keyes (1921–1942) was much more obviously a poet, but the neo-Romantic tradition in which he began to write, which was popular in the wartime Oxford where he was educated, allowed him to develop some of his worst faults—straining for effect, literariness, and an empty sort of evocation summed up in his frequent use of 'O' ('O it is such long learning', 'O it is glory', 'O far away', 'O never come again'). Lewis and Keyes were, at the time of their death, the most highly praised of the 'war poets' (a term which meant much less in the Second than in the First World War, since the implicit feeling among most poets seemed to be that Wilfred Owen had said everything worth saying about war itself). Douglas and Allison were, and are, much less well known. Douglas (1920–1944), who took part in the North African campaign, is a poet of the desert—Egypt, the look and feel of sand, the extreme featurelessness of landscape and climate. Almost everything he wrote had direct relevance to the strange life he was living, as is apparent in his poem 'Words':

> For instance this stooping man, the bones of whose face are
> like the hollow birds' bones, is a trap for words.
> And the pockmarked house bleached by the glare
> whose insides war has dried out like gourds
> attracts words . . .

One wonders whether he could have developed beyond this narrow reference of sensation, within which he worked perfectly and surely. It is difficult now to recapture both the landscape and the life of which he wrote. Drummond Allison (1921–1943), however, was a much more intellectual poet, whose work relied little on places or on the particular atmosphere of the time. He had, within the intellectual framework, a vein of fantasy which produced some of his best poems, including the only one of his which is at all well known—'The Brass Horse', of which this is the first stanza:

> Never presume that in this marble stable
> Furnished with imitation stalactites,
> Withheld from any manger and unable
> To stamp impatient hooves or show the whites
> Of eyes whose lids are fixed, on sulky nights
> He asks himself no questions, has no doubt
> What he a brazen engine is about.

Allison, I feel, had more poetic raw-material, more technical promise, than Lewis, Keyes or Douglas; yet the one slim volume of poems collected after his death looks as if it may well be forgotten.

CHAPTER TEN

Edwin Muir, Robert Graves, William Empson

In all ages there have been some poets who have immediately become fashionable, while others have worked equally well, or better, in obscurity before finally winning recognition. Thus the work of the Auden group made a sudden impact while the poets were still only in their early twenties. Muir, Graves and Empson, however, have until fairly recently been better known, perhaps, for other literary work than their poetry—Muir for his translations of Kafka, Graves for his novels, and Empson for his criticism. It was not until seven or eight years ago that a younger generation of poets, dissatisfied with the characteristic work of the 1930s and 40s, turned to the poetry of these three, discovered them as poets, and learned lessons from them which have helped to shape the attitudes and the manners I describe in Chapter Eleven.

Edwin Muir (1887–1959) described in *An Autobiography* the long and painful journey he made before he could even begin to write poetry. Born on one of the remote islands in the Orkneys, and then plunged, while little more than a child, into a dreary life of menial jobs in Glasgow, he was at first wounded, rather than educated, by life. These mental wounds, which tortured him for years with extraordinary dreams, were gradually healed, partly by his extremely fortunate marriage, partly by his poetry. But, beginning late, he found great difficulty in expressing himself adequately in verse:

> I had no training; I was too old to submit myself to contemporary influences; and I had acquired in Scotland a deference towards ideas which made my entry into poetry difficult. Though my imagination had begun to work, I had no technique by which I could give expression to it. There were the rhythms of English poetry on the one hand, the images in my mind on the other. All I could do at the start was to force the one, creaking and complaining, into the mould of the other . . . I began to write poetry simply because what I wanted to say could not have gone properly into prose. I wanted so much to say it that I had no thought left to study the form in which alone it could be said.

In his *Collected Poems*, Muir omitted a great deal of his early work; but among the few surviving examples of what he was writing in about 1925, there are poems such as 'Childhood', 'Horses' and 'Ballad of Hector in Hades' which are as good as anything he ever wrote, and are stylistically very little different from those he wrote later. The Hector poem is particularly typical, drawing as it does on both traditional myth and personal experience. Muir has written of the influence which his childhood has had on his poetry:

> These years (of childhood) had come alive, after being forgotten for so long, and when I wrote about horses they were my father's plough-horses as I saw them when I was four or five; and a poem on Achilles pursuing Hector round the walls of Troy was really a resuscitation of the afternoon when I ran away, in real terror, from another boy as I returned from school.

And this memory is authentically described, grafted naturally on to the Hector-Achilles story:

The grasses puff a little dust
 Where my footsteps fall.
I cast a shadow as I pass
 The little wayside wall.

The strip of grass on either hand
 Sparkles in the light;
I only see that little space
 To the left and to the right.

And in that space our shadows run,
 His shadow there and mine,
The little flowers, the tiny mounds,
 The grasses frail and fine.

Many of Muir's poems have their origin in, and move in the world of, dream and reverie, a fact which might make one think they would be vague and insubstantial; but the reverse is true. What was most remarkable about him was his clarity of vision and purity of expression in describing or meditating on subjects which turn from abstract into concrete in his hands. Above all, Time is the central character in his poems—a force which is a wheel rather than a river, turning again and again, and always moving through a predestined course:

There is a road that turning always
 Cuts off the country of Again.
Archers stand there on every side
 And as it runs time's deer is slain,
 And lies where it has lain . . .

There the beginning finds the end
 Before beginning ever can be,
And the great runner never leaves
 The starting and the finishing tree,
 The budding and the fading tree.

His work is full of journeys, voyages, races and returns; indeed, he has written at different times three separate poems called 'The Return'. The paradox in these poems is that man thinks he is continually moving forward on 'the great road' of Time, yet always finds himself returning to the point from where he started. Muir personifies this recurrence in different ways: sometimes the Greeks returning from Troy, sometimes Ulysses come back after his wandering, sometimes an old man looking back at his life and re-living it by remembering it, sometimes the poet himself returning to the Orkneys of his childhood. In his early and middle poems, Time is also the annihilator, the insuperable force which makes all our ideas of reality meaningless. But in his middle fifties Muir became a Christian, and since then Time has been the bond which links us with 'a Child, a God . . . a Birth, a Death'; man's birth and death are given significance because they mark the two poles of existence which Christ, too, experienced in his life on earth:

> Make me to see and hear that I may know
> This journey and the place towards which I go;
> For a beginning and an end are mine
> Surely, and have their sign
> Which I and all in the earth and the heavens show.
> Teach me to know.

In Muir's poetry, parables or symbolic stories are very common. Classical Greek myth, the Siegfried legend, the Arthurian cycle and Biblical Old Testament stories are drawn on, but also certain archetypes which have no firm or defined place in existing literature. 'The Combat' is a good example of this. The scene is carefully and closely described, as are the combatants and their action, yet the 'meaning' of it all is left deliberately open and inexplicable. Each reader will make his own interpretation of the struggle; the strong and the weak, evil and good, endlessly pitted in a clash of force against a passive resistance which always, somehow, manages to survive. From the start, the scene is put outside normal existence ('It was not meant for human eyes'), yet the 'crested animal in his pride' and the 'soft round beast as brown as clay' are described as clearly as if they had been drawn from life.

The forms and language which Muir used were always traditional, and it is partly for this reason, no doubt, that he was neglected for so long; in the words of Michael Roberts (who thereby excluded his work from the original version of *The Faber Book of Modern Verse*), he had not 'been compelled to make any notable development of poetic technique'. Leafing quickly through the *Collected Poems*, one notices a large number of quatrains and other regularly organised stanzas, a certain amount of blank verse, a general predominance of rhyme, and a liking for lyrical metres. But, taking more than a summary glance, one sees how freshly he works within this framework; even the archaisms have their place in the 'timelessness' of his scheme. Because his movement is easy and his language transparent (rather than opaque, like that of Dylan Thomas, for example), what he says is achieved with the minimum fuss. And it would be wrong to call Muir simply a traditional poet (he has sometimes absurdly been lumped with Blunden, a very different and much less relevant figure), for his search, his anxiety, his unquietness, his problems in general, are basically very much of our time; look, for example, at his fine poem 'The Interrogation', which probably stems from his eye-witness view of Czechoslovakia in 1948:

> We cannot choose
> Answer or action here,
> Though still the careless lovers saunter by
> And the thoughtless field is near.

> We are on the very edge,
> Endurance almost done,
> And still the interrogation is going on.

The questioners, the questioned, and the heedless world beyond the two is of the present day; yet the strength of the poem is that it could as easily be about any frontier at any time of stress and barbarism, and it is the lack of particular reference which makes it so frighteningly effective. Muir saw today's newspaper as yesterday's history.

ROBERT GRAVES

Muir, as I said before, began writing poetry late; Robert Graves (b. 1895) made an exceptionally early start. He made a vow at the age of fifteen never to compromise himself in his vocation as a poet, a vow which would not be unusual except for the fact that he has kept it all his life. More than almost anyone else in this century, he has been a professional poet and, even if his poetry were not as remarkable as it is, the integrity of his devotion, his ceaseless hard work, and his uncompromising and critical attitude to his own and others' writing would make him respected.

His earliest verse—written in his late 'teens and early twenties—was no more memorable than any of the Georgian poetry of the period. But his experience as a young officer in the First World War both disturbed and toughened him. As Martin Seymour-Smith has written:

> The First World War gave Graves a deep personal shock, from which, at some level, he perhaps never quite recovered. It destroyed, as the title of his autobiography (*Goodbye To All*

That) suggests, his belief in the existence of traditional stable values in European, and English, society. It gave him a sense of isolation and insecurity. It left him with images of pain and horror, which bit deep into his mind. At the same time, at a compensating level, it left him with a soldier's pride and a soldier's admiration for dour, staunch, disciplined courage.

To Graves, the answer to his neurosis was apparently work; in 1925, for example, he published six books, and eight in 1927. Yet much of what he was doing at this time was fragmentary; though everything he wrote—both in verse and prose—had a tart, individual flavour, there seemed to be little 'body'; many of his poems, in particular, were simply pieces of fancy or whimsy.

However, in 1929 he left England to settle in Mallorca (one of the Balearic Islands in the Mediterranean), and from that time on his gifts have grown and matured. His self-imposed isolation from English literary life has left him free to work out his own poetic salvation and to take an idiosyncratic view of what everyone else is writing. In Mallorca, too, he met Laura Riding, the American poet, and collaborated with her in many ventures. Most important of all was the mutual influence of each other's poems and, as is often the case, the work of the less important poet served as a necessary stimulus to the better. Laura Riding's work has never been well known, but I guarantee that if some of her poems were read out to a competent audience, nine out of ten would say that they were by Graves. Yet what is abstract and delicate in Laura Riding becomes concrete and tough in Graves; his poetic tone of voice is wry, ironical, reserved, and yet immensely strong.

His themes have varied, but the dialectic clash at the centre of almost every poem has remained the same; a clash between love and hate, between two contrary aspects of love, between innocence and experience, or between the haunting presences of the past set against the reality of the present. And this clash or dualism is frequently seen on the level of childhood or childish myth, as in both 'Warning to Children' and 'Lollocks'. The complex, nightmarish face which reality can sometimes turn towards one is minimised by making a game of it; outside the game lie the terrors:

> Children, if you dare to think
> Of the greatness, rareness, muchness,
> Fewness of this precious only
> Endless world in which you say
> You live, you think of things like this:
> Blocks of slate enclosing dappled
> Red and green, enclosing tawny
> Yellow nets, enclosing white
> And black acres of dominoes . . .

These unconnected childish properties endlessly repeat themselves, like a series of Chinese boxes each within each—and what is at the bottom of it all (i.e. what is the quintessence of reality)? Whatever it is, Graves suggests, we can never find it, even if we 'untie the string'; nor, perhaps, is it relevant to want to find it. In the same way, the Lollocks are inexplicable; all we can do is blame them for their daily horrors, and attempt to keep them at bay by being neat and orderly in our personal affairs. Men, being rational, deny their presence, but 'suffer the more, / Both in neck and belly'; women, being irrational, are in league with the unreason of the Lollocks. Finally,

> Sovereign against Lollocks,
> Are hard broom and soft broom,
> To well comb the hair,
> To well brush the shoe,
> And to pay every debt
> So soon as it's due.

What is apparent in both these poems is a simultaneous attraction towards and revulsion from extravaganza. This mixture of comedy and horror has its place in English literature, from *Alice in Wonderland* to the ghost stories of M. R. James. It is found more light-heartedly in Graves's 'Welsh Incident', which is no more and no less than it appears to be—a fantastic anecdote, deliberately wrenched out of context, which shows how sympathetic Graves is to Celtic exaggeration and fancy (a more serious side of this appears in Graves's 're-creations' of ancient Welsh and Irish magical poems). Graves would no doubt explain it by pointing out that there is Irish and Scottish blood in his veins. The Celtic races are known for the blurred line they draw between dream and reality, between spirit and substance. But it should be noticed that in 'Welsh Incident' Graves is, above all, *laughing* at gullibility and exaggeration.

Another of his themes is transience and the remorselessness of Time in its devouring of love and beauty; unlike Muir, he is more concerned with the effects, rather than the idea, of Time. Body and soul pull in different directions, and our clumsy physical expression of love is 'tainted', but there is still a quality of joy in that very expression, feeble and impermanent as it is. Thus he addresses Love in 'O Love In Me':

> Be warm, enjoy the season, lift your head,
> Exquisite in the pulse of tainted blood,
> That shivering glory not to be despised.
>
> Take your delight in momentariness,
> Walk between dark and dark, a shining space
> With the grave's narrowness, though not its peace.

Time, too, can have its strange reversals: who is truly living and who is truly dead? Again, the physical being tugs at the spiritual, as in 'To Bring the Dead to Life':

> To bring the dead to life
> Is no great magic.
> Few are wholly dead:
> Blow on a dead man's embers
> And a live flame will start.
>
> Let his forgotten griefs be now,
> And now his withered hopes;
> Subject your pen to his handwriting
> Until it prove as natural
> To sign his name as yours.

So the poem continues, advising the living to adopt exactly all the characteristics which made (in Hopkins's word) the 'inscape' of the dead man; his manner of walking, his language, his clothes, his bodily disabilities. But then 'the greedy revenant' will return, and you must

> reckon
> That the grave which housed him
> May not be empty now:
> You in his spotted garments
> Must yourself lie wrapped.

Above all, it is human love which suffers from the ravages and dishonesties of Time; love, which existed 'before words were', is quickly destroyed by words, which, spoken or written down, are in time. Yet, though language destroys love, lovers cannot do without it:

> Wise after the event, by love withered,
> A 'never more!' most frantically

> Sorrow and shame would proclaim
> Such as, they'd swear, never before were:
> True lovers even in this.

Such a poem shows Graves's strange mixture of cynicism and tenderness, a union of emotions he often brings to his love poetry. It is a romantic attitude, very ready (as are most romantic attitudes) to be disillusioned, but aware that this self-deception and fickleness are themselves part of the variousness and richness of existence. The fact that life (and thus love) is brief, forces us to recognise Time, but Graves sees that it is human to ignore it, and sympathises with the fault because it *is* human; for, despite his stress on 'magic', he is a humanist:

> What monster's proof against that lovesome pair,
> Old age and childhood, seals of Time,
> His sorrowful vagueness?
>
> Or will not render him the accustomed thanks,
> Humouring age with filial flowers,
> Childhood with pebbles?

The question is rhetorical; Time claims all things with 'its sorrowful vagueness', and cannot—though many attempt it— be ignored. Wisdom and breadth of experience are here as wide and as apparent as they are in Yeats.

WILLIAM EMPSON

William Empson (b. 1906) first attracted some attention as a poet while he was still an undergraduate, with a group of poems in the anthology *Cambridge Poetry 1929*. The biographical fact that he was trained at the university both as a mathematician and as a student of English literature helps one to see the basis on which his poems have been built; they are the work of a man accustomed to think logically (in abstract terms and symbolically), who is also particularly attracted to the Metaphysical poets of the seventeenth century. While he was writing these early poems, he was also working on his pioneer book of literary analysis, *Seven Types of Ambiguity*, and the teasing, fine-drawn quality of his mind is evident in both. Indeed, Empson's ideas about poetic ambiguity are one of the pointers into his poetry.

Some of his early poems are, quite frankly, impenetrable. What, for example, is one to make of this, despite seventeen lines of notes which Empson appends at the back of the book?

> Spears pierce its desert basin, the long dawn:
> Tower, noon, all cliquant, dock-side cranes, sag-fruited:
> And, sand-born weight, brief by waste sand upborne,
> Leave, gulfed, ere night, the bare plain, deeper rooted.

The fussy, intrusive punctuation here breaks the stanza up into fragments, and words by themselves are being forced into doing more than they decently can. One gets a hint as to how Empson writes, and why he fails in such a passage as this, in a note to another poem, where he says of an idea (an ambiguity, in fact) that he 'failed to get that into the line'; one has a mental picture of Empson assiduously loading every rift with ore. Yet elsewhere in these poems he manages to keep maximum allusiveness and compactness, and at the same time lets enough light show between the lines so that one can read and understand them. In 'To an Old Lady', for example, he illustrates the poem's central figure by references to *King Lear*, the movement and substance of planets, the habits of bees and the fact that the universe is finite but unbounded, yet he does all this without any hint of preciosity or irrelevance:

> Ripeness is all; her in her cooling planet
> Revere; do not presume to think her wasted.
> Project her no projectile, plan nor man it;
> Gods cool in turn, by the sun long outlasted . . .
>
> Stars how much further from me fill my night.
> Strange that she too should be inaccessible,
> Who shares my sun. He curtains her from sight,
> And but in darkness is she visible.

The central point in Empson's poetry, far more important than his eagerness to draw abstruse scientific analogies or wring the last drop of juice out of an ambiguity, can be found in one of his notes to the poem 'Bacchus' (a poem which in itself is hardly worth bothering about, unless one has a taste for strenuous crossword puzzles): 'Life involves maintaining oneself between contradictions that can't be solved by analysis.' It is with this theme in mind that he has written some of his best poems, both conversational ('Reflection from Rochester', 'Courage means Running') and highly-wrought ('Aubade', 'This Last Pain', 'Missing Dates'). One of the most astonishing things about him is that he has projected such tricky philosophical thinking into forms which one would have thought would have been unworkable for the purpose—*terza rima*, the villanelle, the aubade; the first (despite, or perhaps because of, Dante) has never really taken root in England, while the second two are delicate Provençal verse-schemes which have, in England at any rate, always been used for trivial subjects and tinkling music. But with Empson the repetitions and inversions of these forms become, in turn, menacing, wistful, savage, resigned. 'Aubade', for example, is a laconic meditation, a discussion poised between the repeated antitheses 'It seemed the best thing to be up and go' and 'The heart of standing is you cannot fly'—or, to paraphrase these lines, 'Flight seemed the only answer' and 'The essence of courage is that, whether you like it or not, you have to stand your ground.' These refrains yoke together the disparate elements of earthquake, adultery and war, so that the whole poem is working on at least three levels. Beginning with the real earthquake (in Japan), it moves on to his own insecurity, in this particular human relationship and in the world's chaos, for which the earthquake is a convenient symbol; it cannot be escaped from, either by physical flight or dreams:

> I slept, and blank as that I would yet lie.
> Till you have seen what a threat holds below,
> The heart of standing is you cannot fly.

Bodily escape, through movement or lust ('A bedshift flight to a Far Eastern sky'), bring one back, paradoxically, only to where one started from:

> But as to risings, I can tell you why.
> It is on contradiction that they grow.
> It seemed the best thing to be up and go.
> Up was the heartening and the strong reply,
> The heart of standing is we cannot fly.

'Up', therefore, to face those things from which 'we cannot fly': contradictions demand courage. This moral honesty, or 'wise patience' as he applies it in 'Courage means Running', is one of several qualities which make Empson a poet listened to and admired by the younger literary generation in England, tired of slogans and dogma. It, rather than his much-discussed 'puzzle interest' and 'metaphysical wit', is a quality worth learning from.

CHAPTER ELEVEN

Poetry since 1950

In October 1954 an article called 'In the Movement' appeared in the English weekly magazine, *The Spectator*. It was a deliberately provocative, almost truculent, account of certain tendencies which the writer of the article had noticed in the work of several young poets and novelists during the past few years. The writer did not pretend that these tendencies had at that time formed a cohesive whole, but he gave the impression that the work he was discussing formed part of something which could honestly be called a literary move-ment, with a common style, subject matter and general way of looking at, and writing about, life. The Movement (as it simply came to be known) was seen to have its ancestors: 'Genuflections towards Dr. Leavis and Professor Empson, admiration for people whom the Thirties by-passed, Orwell above all (and, for another example, Mr. Robert Graves) are indeed signs by which you may recognise the Movement.' Since then, a sort of 'programme' anthology has been pub-lished (*New Lines*, edited by Robert Conquest). One can scarcely open a literary magazine nowadays without finding some mention of the Movement, or some reference to a writer supposed to be connected with it. Whatever it is, it seems to have been accepted as the representative mode of the present decade.

Conquest, in his introduction to *New Lines*, has this to say about it:

> If one had briefly to distinguish the poetry of the fifties from its
> predecessors, I believe the most important general point would

be that it submits to no great systems of theoretical constructs nor agglomerations of unconscious demands. It is free from both mystical and logical compulsions and—like modern philosophy—is empirical in its attitude to all that comes. This reverence for the real person or event is, indeed, a part of the general intellectual ambience (in so far as that is not blind or retrogressive) of our time. One might, without stretching matters too far, say that George Orwell with his principle of real, rather than ideological, honesty, exerted, even though indirectly, one of the major influences on modern poetry.

The reaction was thus against both the socially-engaged, politically-committed poetry of the 'Macspaunday' poets of the 1930s and also against the emotional, free-association work of Dylan Thomas, George Barker and those poets of the 1940s who achieved an overwrought Romanticism in their poetry, manufactured from some of the most ex- aggerated mannerisms of Thomas and Barker. But what really replaced these attitudes? Conquest's wordy and slightly pompous 'statement of belief' points us towards 'empiricism', but that is not a term one can often fruitfully illustrate by turning to the poems themselves, as one can turn to, say, Orwell's *Homage to Catalonia* and call the attitudes expressed there empirical. But 'real honesty'—that takes us nearer the truth, I think; for these poets scrupulously refuse to say what they don't mean, and are sometimes almost painfully con- cerned to record the exact shades of their responses. Their honesty very often expresses itself in terms of bluff common sense, in easy and colloquial language; this is perhaps another part of Orwell's influence.

But these poets are among the first to admit that honesty and clarity are not enough in themselves. Some of their published statements show this straighforwardly enough. Kingsley Amis: 'Their great deficiency [i.e. the newer poets] is meagreness and triviality of subject-matter'; Donald Davie: 'English poetry today, it seems to me, is at its best far more elegant and workmanlike than it was ten years ago, and also more humane; but it is rather unambitious, too limited in its scope, insufficiently various and adventurous'; Enright: 'Clarity may in itself be a pleasant change after an over-dose of obscurity—but it can have no real meaning unless it is being clear *about* something.' These poets all felt a revulsion against what John Wain called 'the punch-drunk random "romantic" scribblers' whose verses filled a great number of the pages of *Poetry London* and *Poetry Quarterly* during the years from about 1940 to 50. Many of them are academics— educated at, and later teaching at, the universities (of the nine poets in Conquest's anthology, six are, or at some time have been, university lecturers in English literature, and two are librarians in university towns, closely tied to the universities); thus they have been trained to think critically about literature, and it is significant that the leading younger poets are at the same time some of the leading younger critics. Davie, Enright, Holloway and Wain have all written books of literary criticism, and they—with Amis—are frequent reviewers in the weekly magazines.

This critical awareness has itself probably been an inhibiting factor, limiting the scope and ambition of the poets' designs. An artist's critical faculties are at least as delicate in their mechanism as, if not more than, his creative energies; the balance between the two is kept only with difficulty. If the excesses of 'a high emotional temperature and a heavy dramatisation of the poet's personality' (as John Wain typifies some of the characteristics of much verse of the 1940s) are avoided, the alternative pitfalls may be a frigid decorum and a studious impersonality—pitfalls into which most of these poets have dropped at one time or another. Still, it is as

unfair to treat the poets of the 1950s as a homogeneous group
as it is roundly to condemn the poets of the 1940s—after all,
whatever criticism may legitimately be levelled at the
general standard of the previous decade, it was in those years
that Eliot, Muir and Dylan Thomas produced some of their
best work.

Kingsley Amis (b. 1922) and John Wain (b. 1925) are
frequently spoken of in the same breath, almost as if they
formed a composite poet; indeed, they have characteristics
in common—a shared college and university background,
an impatience with 'sensibility' (as they find it in, say, Jane
Austen and Virginia Woolf), a slangy, 'common man'
attitude to life and literature—but their poems have definite
and definable differences. Wain has always been much more
influenced by Empson, using very commonly the forms
(*terza rima* and the villanelle) which Empson had more or less
patented anew in the 1930s; and Wain's essay on Empson,
'Ambiguous Gifts', in the last number of *Penguin New
Writing* (published in 1950), was instrumental in drawing
attention to the lessons that could be learned from this
neglected (at that time) poet. Indeed, within the strict limits
of the Empsonian forms Wain is at his best; elsewhere, in
such freer poems as 'Cameo', 'Patriotic Poem', 'Usefulness of
Light', and in his two sonnets, he is much less successful.
Wain commands best what G. S. Fraser has called 'the bold
Drydenic line'—iambic pentameter, generally end-stopped,
so that each line becomes a separate rhetorical unit.
Thus:

> Beyond the passion lies the deep content
> and We only utter what we lightly know
> and It is a lie that time can heal a wound
> and It is not only for escape we fly.

These four lines are all moral statements, and that is precisely what Wain's poems generally are. They take an idea, in the form of a statement, and examine it, succinctly and deliberately. 'On Reading Love Poetry in the Dentist's Waiting Room', for example, sets in antithesis the words *joy* (as applied to the feelings of the lovers in the poem he is reading) and *pain* (as applied, deliberately trivially, to his sensation in the dentist's waiting room), and plots the first through until it is identified with the second:

> Yet in some silent sphere beyond the grave
> Their pleasure and my pain shall be as one,
> When all sensation, like a breaking wave,
>
> Shall sink into the pebbles and be gone.
> And then their anguish shall be my fruition.

Their 'written joy' becomes a solace for his minor pain. The trouble about this sort of poem is that it can too easily remain on merely a literary level. Another danger—present in this poem—is that the strict *cadence* of the form makes it possible for vague or arbitrary thinking to masquerade as strict *logic*; thus, in the version of this poem printed in an anthology the seventeenth line reads

> And then their anguish shall be my fruition,

whereas in Wain's volume *A Word Carved on a Sill* (published a year after the anthology) it reads

> And then my anguish shall be their fruition.

The revision shows how arbitrary the apparently explicit statement is.

Amis is a much more various poet, experimenting with

many different forms and themes; and his mentors have obviously been Auden and Graves, both of them versatile writers. He can achieve the clipped, serious rhetoric of 'Masters' (one of the finest poems, I think, written by any of the poets mentioned in this chapter) and the flippant, colloquial shrewdness of 'Something Nasty in the Bookshop'; the rich, Gravesian particularity of 'Against Romanticism', and the wry, disturbing wit of 'The Voice of Authority'. Amis, like Wain, is a poet of common morality, but unlike Wain he does not, on the whole, make explicit moral statements, preferring to imply them; it is this that makes 'Something Nasty in the Bookshop' such an effective poem—the supercilious and off-hand sentiments expressed in the first eight stanzas are immediately exploded by the implication of the last stanza; the sting is all in the tail:

> Deciding this, we can forget those times
>   We sat up half the night
> Chock-full of love, crammed with bright thoughts, names,
>   rhymes,
>   And couldn't write.

In 'Nocturne', too, the moral statement is muted; one is led astray (and is meant to be led astray) by the reference to the Watch Committee. The 'animal' nature of the people making love and of the drunk sailor is seen as ambiguous—something more and less than animal; no actual judgment is made. These unpolished edges in Amis's poems are, I think, more effective than the smooth surfaces in Wain's. There is pleasure in what is left unsaid.

Smoothness and elegance are immediately obvious qualities in Donald Davie's poetry (b. 1920). They are qualities which Davie admires in eighteenth century verse, and he has drawn attention to this connection with his own work:

> I have tried to get force into my poems, not by concentration of highly figurative language, nor by dislocation of traditional syntax, but by making syntax, while flawlessly correct, as compact and rapid as possible, in the manner of some eighteenth century poets.

And, more sardonically, in 'Homage to William Cowper', he has called himself

> A pasticheur of late-Augustan styles.

But one should not take these overt attitudes too seriously, nor imagine that Davie is simply an apostle of elegance. He has given a more energetic indication of what he demands from form in his poem 'Zip!':

> Lines should be hoops that, vibrantly at rest,
> Devolve like cables as the switches trip,
> Each syllable entailing all the rest,
> And rhymes that strike, exploding like a whip.

This is the poet-critic *par excellence*—experiencing form not simply with the head, but also with the nerves and the heart. Though the quatrain I have just quoted is strict and regular, it has tremendous compressed energy. Such compressed energy is characteristic of Davie's poetry at its best. In its less successful moments it goes powdery and dry, or—when he attempts the colloquial—prim and 'donnish'. An example of the latter fault can be found in his otherwise fine poem, 'The Evangelist'. This is a poem about the poet and someone else (perhaps his wife) attending church and listening to a sermon by an emotional evangelical preacher, who irritates the poet with his carefully mannered performance. Everyone else, even the poet's companion, is moved by the preacher:

> You round upon me, generously keen:
> The man, you say, is patently sincere.
> Because he is so eloquent, you mean?
> That test was never patented, my dear.

The play on 'patently' and 'patented' seems to me to be merely clever, and even offensive; and the smug little aside, 'my dear', adds to the patronising condescension. The balance between wit and levity has been lost. Yet this perhaps—sensing the complexity of approach in the poem—is intentional, for it ends:

> If, when he plays upon our sympathies,
> I'm pleased to be fastidious, and you
> To be inspired, the vice in it is this:
> Each does us credit, and we know it too.

It is this razor-edge quality which I referred to when, earlier in this chapter, I said that these poets are sometimes 'almost painfully concerned to record the exact shades of their responses'. It can be found, too, in Davie's 'The Garden Party'; the poet's envy, pleasure, nostalgia and bitterness are extremely subtly mixed, and it would be wrong to take the last line

> But theirs is all the youth we might have had

as the dominant theme. The situation, he admits, is 'contrived' —and what is implied is that the poet's sentiments may similarly be contrived.

Philip Larkin (b. 1922) has been more widely and whole-heartedly praised than any other of the poets in this chapter. His first full-scale book of poems, *The Less Deceived* (published in 1955), contains a selection of the work he has written since 1945. These poems are not, at a first glance, highly-wrought, yet their organisation and craftsmanship are extremely sure. Their range, too, is much wider than that of Amis's, Wain's or Davie's poems; many of them deal with subjects which could easily have been sentimentalised—a girl's photograph album, the idea of a girl's maiden name, old racehorses which have been 'put to grass', myxomatosis (the disease which has been deliberately spread among rabbits, in an attempt to exterminate them, and which has a slowly paralysing, rather than a quickly killing, effect on them). He has the ability to feel his way into a complex emotion or resolution by beginning with a concrete situation, perhaps a quite trivial one, and then to use that situation as a sort of parable, implicit in his resolution. Such a poem is 'Next, Please', which starts with the simple idea that, like Mr. Micawber, we are always 'waiting for something to turn up'. And Larkin uses as his image of these elusive hopes the proverbial ship (i.e. as in the phrase 'When my ship comes in'); the difference is that this 'armada of promises' is concretely drawn, a literal fleet appearing, and then disappearing, on the horizon. But none of these is 'our ship', only the ship of destiny or fate which follows behind us, carrying oblivion with it. Notice the contrast between the easy, conversational first stanza

> Always too eager for the future, we
> Pick up bad habits of expectancy.
> Something is always approaching; every day
> *Till then* we say . . .

and the superbly-controlled foreboding of the last
stanza:

> Only one ship is seeking us, a black-
> Sailed unfamiliar, towing at her back
> A huge and birdless silence. In her wake
> No waters breed or break.

In the same way, he is a master of the balance between
concrete and abstract, as, for example, in 'The Less Deceived',
which draws on an account of the rape of a drugged girl
given in the mid-nineteenth century social study, Mayhew's
London Labour and the London Poor. The abandoned grief of the
girl lying on the bed merges into the vicarious grief of the
poet; the first is put concretely, the second in impersonal
but sensitive abstractions:

> What can be said,
> Except that suffering is exact, but where
> Desire takes charge, readings will grow erratic?

The poem then moves to its balance of grief on the one hand,
self-deception on the other, where the actual scene and its
meaning complement one another:

> For you would hardly care
> That you were less deceived, out on that bed,
> Than he was, stumbling up the breathless stair
> To burst into fulfilment's desolate attic.

Larkin's longest poem, 'Church Going' (included in *New
Lines*), keeps this balance of concrete and abstract particularly
well, moving from particular to general in a way that recalls

Yeats in 'A Prayer for my Daughter' and 'Among School-children'. Larkin's humanity is apparent in every line he writes, and perhaps what is particularly appealing about it is that it seems the humanity of the ordinary, decent man—if the ordinary, decent man had the self-awareness and skill to make poems of what he felt.

The poetry of Elizabeth Jennings (b. 1926) is best read in bulk, for she has constructed a method—almost a world—of observation and meditation which is remarkably coherent, but which in isolated poems tends sometimes to seem vague and remote. There is a seriousness about her work which is more severe than in any of the poets I have so far discussed. I am not implying that her poetry is cold or inhuman, but its sensitiveness is far purer than the gritty circumstance which lies, like the sand round a pearl, in Amis, Wain and the others. She relies more wholly on perfection of diction and movement, and what she explores—states of mind about identity, love, landscapes, memory—is a continual capture and analysis of the elusive. This can be seen most simply, perhaps, in her poem 'For a Child Born Dead', where the purity and innocence of the death moves, without any explicit moralising, to an awareness of the purity of the resultant grief; the child is beyond any manufactured grief, because there are no memories which could distort what has happened:

> But there is nothing now to mar
> Your clear refusal of our world.
> Not in our memories can we mould
> You or distort your character.
> Then all our consolation is
> That grief can be as pure as this.

Another feature of her work, in particular many of her earlier poems, to which she draws attention, is her special use of allegory 'to reveal meanings and significances on various levels'; such poems as 'Bell-Ringer', 'Fishermen', and elsewhere 'The Climbers', 'The Geologist', 'The Island', take people or places as parables of thought or behaviour. 'Bell-Ringer', for instance, is not only about a man who rings the church-bells of the town, and thus in some sense controls the movements of the townspeople, but is more deeply concerned with the effect of one's single will and influence on others. This is a method of which she acknowledges Edwin Muir is the master, and indeed Muir has helped her not only to find that method but also has influenced her in her gentle, unhurried language; though she is more complex than Muir. Anne Ridler (in her Introduction to Elizabeth Jennings's first book) was right to point out that the line 'Seekers who are their own discovery' sums up the subject matter of many of the poems, and also the method, for they are not resolved pieces of emotional thought turned into verse, but rather accounts of exploration before any goal is reached, resting-places on the way on a journey of discovery.

Self-discovery, of a more energetic and often more brutal sort, is one of Thom Gunn's (b. 1929) central themes. The poems in his first book, *Fighting Terms*, are mainly concerned with love, but with love as a battle, political or military, involving strategy and hard-headed discipline. The very title of his book is an indication of his manner and his preoccupations: the manner, tough and cynical: the preoccupations, life as a struggle, a pattern of advance and retreat in a ceaseless war of skirmishes across the landscape of love:

> Shall I be John a Gaunt and with my band
> Of mad bloods pass in one spectacular dash,
> Fighting before and after, through your land . . . ?

Yet often he is tired of the struggle:

> Tactics commit me falsely, what I want
> Is not the raising of a siege but this:
> Honour in the town at peace.

They are poems of doubt and bewilderment, but always expressed in firm and deliberate terms:

> Searching thoroughly, I did not see what I wanted.
> What I wanted would have been what I found.

His later poems, several of which are included in *New Lines*, have ranged more widely, but the manner is still recognisably the same; indeed, one critic has said that 'his is the first really original voice to have appeared in English poetry for a long time.' His most ambitious poem, and one of his best, is 'On the Move', which explores the idea of un-motivated action and violence, taking as its symbol the tough 'boys' on motor-cycles who personify this idea, who 'almost hear a meaning in their noise'. Their restlessness is approved, because 'One is always nearer by not keeping still.' This is typical of what seems to be Gunn's philosophy, which is more closely in keeping with the 'empiricism' mentioned in Conquest's Introduction than any of his companions in *New Lines*:

> Much is unknowable.
> No problem shall be faced
> Until the problem is;
> I, born to fog, to waste,
> Walk through hypothesis,
> An individual.

It is particularly difficult to see why D. J. Enright (b. 1920) has ever been included among the Movement poets (though one questions the placing of Elizabeth Jennings there as well); because in many ways he seems to be as 'socially-conscious' as any of the 1930s poets. The difference, I suppose, is that he is never doctrinaire, taking each event and place as it comes, bringing to these events and places his common-sense morality (which is often moral indignation) and his amused, and sometimes bitter, irony. I mention 'places' advisedly, since he is a firm delineator of the features which make injustice and inequality different in different places. His poems range round England, the Mediterranean, Egypt and Japan; and those dealing with Japan are particularly successful. They approach the real problems of the country without any received opinions, except those of common humanity, and contrast callousness and hypocrisy with actual and unrelieved suffering:

> The peasants have salvaged their cabbages; the block
> of flats is nearly as ready as its tenants; somewhere
> someone saves a child from a swollen river,
> and really means it—
> > the critics in their studies, collate as ever
> their absences of meanings, unvexing and unvexed—
> > but the grass waves high on the road again,
> and the roots refer to the text

What is immediately apparent here, as elsewhere in Enright's poems, is the looseness of structure, the conversational and even flippant tone (e.g. 'roots' taken in a punning sense, applying both to language and to the roots of the grass—a much more obvious, and deliberately more lighweight, pun than anything in Empson; the ambiguity does not have to be dug out with a delicate instrument). The same harsh contrast

of the great and the small appears in 'The Short Life of
Kazuo Yamamoto', the laconic account (taken from a
newspaper report) of a thirteen-year-old shoeshine boy's
suicide:

> Elsewhere the great ones have their headaches, too,
> As they grapple with those notable tongue-twisters
> Such as Liberation and Oppression.
>   But they were not talking about you,
> Kazuo, who found rat poison cheaper than aspirin.

Yet there is no resignation in this attitude, but resilience.
Self-mockingly, he looks at his subject-matter and his indignation (in 'Busy-Body under a Cherry Tree'), and finds
that the tree

>   Reminds the busy-body . . .
> that the cherry's body all year round is busy
> Against one week of showered gifts without advice,
> For it is silent, for its deeds suffice.

At the base of his indignation is not only a sense of humour
and a sense of justice, but a sense of balance.

There is no space here to consider some of the other poets
who have been—whether advisedly or not—grouped with
the Movement; John Holloway (b. 1920) and Philip Oakes
(b. 1928) seem to me to be among the more interesting,
though Holloway's imagery often appears to be too clogged
and ornate for what he wants to say (an exception is his
'Apollonian Poem', originally published in *New Poems 1953*),
and Oakes is a myth-maker, after the manner of Graves, who
has emotional force which is sometimes spoiled by over-
ingenuity.

There are, of course, a number of young poets who do not

fit into the boundaries of the Movement—vague as those
boundaries are—and who can be called 'romantic', if that
term any longer means anything. Some of them were
grouped together, in deliberate opposition to *New Lines*, in
an anthology called *Mavericks*, edited by Dannie Abse and
Howard Sergeant. The poets included were Anthony Cronin,
J. C. Hall, Michael Hamburger, Vernon Scannell, Jon Silkin,
John Smith, W. Price Turner, David Wright, and Dannie
Abse himself. The general level of *Mavericks* is certainly
lower than that of *New Lines*, but J. C. Hall (b. 1920) and
Jon Silkin (b. 1930) are good poets and should not be smoth-
ered in the squabbling of cliques or obscured by the tying on
of superficial critical labels.

Hall's poetry is very often reminiscent of Muir's, but this
is not a case of simple derivativeness, though Hall has done
much to introduce Muir to a wider public by writing both
the introduction to the *Collected Poems* and a 'Writers and
their Work' pamphlet on him. Such poems of Hall's as 'The
Boy and the Mare' and 'The Duel' obviously spring from
the same areas of imagination and imagery as Muir's:

> Two men face to face:
>   Equally, as they stand,
> Light flashes from the blade
>   Each carries in his hand.
>
> He nearest to me now
>   Grips murder in the right.
> His adversary comes
>   Left-handed to the fight . . .
>
> And as they strike and strike
>   The mirror tinkles down.
> They and the world crash out.
>   Naked I stand alone.

One thing that distinguishes Hall from Muir is that his 'myths' generally seem to be personal in origin, rather than coming from the Bible or the Greek stories. Hall is not an exciting or markedly very original poet, but his elegiac sense and his lyricism are attractive.

Silkin has been compared to D. H. Lawrence, largely because both poets employ animals as symbols of the human condition: but whereas Lawrence almost always used them as emblems to illustrate the gulf between them and humans or between their appearance and their 'meaning' (as in 'Humming-Bird', for example), Silkin uses them as living parables of decency, tolerance and love, creatures removed from ourselves by only a tiny fraction:

> From growing mercy and a moderate love
> Great love for the human animal occurs.

What this implies is a great compassion, a great tenderness for the dumb struggling of all life, whether human or animal; responsibilities begin when such concern becomes a rule of conduct. The technical equipment Silkin uses is crude, often naive, but the crudity and the naivete keep out the worse faults of glibness and over-sophistication; his concern with innocence, with cruelty and with death—large, dangerous themes—is warm and human.

Two interesting poets of a rather earlier generation who began to be recognised in the 1950s are Thomas Blackburn and Charles Causley. Blackburn (b. 1916) is too often apt to fall into the rhythms, the language and even the attitudes of Yeats; but at his best, he transcends the influence and constructs very powerful poems—'The Maze', for example, which is concerned with the myth of Ariadne, Theseus and the Minotaur:

Tonight that thirsting girl glides through the town,
With nervous footsteps from the royal door,
Crushed ivy, liquid music in her mouth,
To mate a beast upon the sea's cold shore . . .

The morning breaks; upon the trampled sand,
Blood crusted to her side, foam in her hair,
She drops blue pebbles from an idle hand,
Sunlight reflected in her calm blank stare.

And then they find her; she can't speak at all,
Giggles and points her tongue, she plays bo-peep,
Crawls crab-like on the earth, begins to weep,
Blasted and burnt out like a terminal.

Causley (b. 1917) has some of the virtues and vices—and
some of the popular appeal, too—of Kipling. He often
writes in ballad form, and always in a racy, direct, unsubtle
way. Sometimes one feels that he is deliberately over-
simplifying, so as to give pace and thrust to his way of
expressing himself. But his simple metrical devices of anapaest
and internal rhyme are effective within their limits, and they
do not try to be more than limited:

Under the willow the willow
    I heard the butcher bird sing,
Come out you fine young fellow
    From under your mother's wing.
I'll show you the magic garden
    That hangs in the beamy air,
The way of the lynx and the angry Sphinx
    And the fun of the freezing fair . . .

The trouble with this sort of writing is that it reduces all
experience, serious and light, satirical and merely gay, to the
same level of expression, so that the passage from 'Recruiting

Drive' which I have just quoted may seem, at a glance, to be no deeper than, say, 'Cowboy Song', which begins

> I come from Salem County
>   Where the silver melons grow,
> Where the wheat is sweet as an angel's feet
>   And the zithering zephyrs blow . . .

Lastly, there are two young poets whose work cannot be linked with the Movement, and who have already shown that they have strength and individuality: Ted Hughes (b. 1930) and Geoffrey Hill (b. 1932). There is great vigour in Hughes's poetry; occasionally it is a vigour which obscures the meaning, a mere show of animal spirits and animal sensibility. But in the better poems, which seem to cohere round a single theme, the imagery becomes direct and purposeful, and not merely fierce and distracting:

> There is no better way to know us
> Than as two wolves, come separately to a wood.
> Now neither's able to sleep—even at a distance
> Distracted by the soft competing pulse
> Of the other; nor able to hunt—at every step
> Looking backwards and sideways, warying to listen
> For the other's slavering rush . . .

Geoffrey Hill is a powerful religious poet in the line of Christopher Smart and Blake, concerned with traditional themes in a strong, sometimes slightly archaic, language; his most impressive poem, 'Genesis', is too long to quote here; but the following poem, 'Merlin', gives some idea of his elegiac quality:

> I will consider the outnumbering dead:
> For they are the husks of what was rich seed.
> Now, should they come together to be fed,
> They would outstrip the locusts' covering tide.

Arthur, Elaine, Mordred: they are all gone
Among the raftered galleries of bone.
By the long barrows of Logres they are made one,
And over their city stands the pinnacled corn.

The final impression, therefore, of the young poets of this decade is that they are not uniform, however much critics, both hostile and friendly, talk about the 'distinctive manner of the 1950s'. The state of poetry seems to me to be healthy, though not particularly conducive to (or at least not producing) greatness. And the condition of minor poetry is perhaps more significant than the occasional, freak, inexplicable appearance of the great poet, who is not produced by conditions but by chance.

Select Bibliography

1. CRITICISM

Auden by Richard Hoggart. Chatto & Windus, 1951.

Auden and After by Francis Scarfe. Routledge, 1942.

Selected Essays by T. S. Eliot. Faber, 1951.

The Art of T. S. Eliot by Helen Gardner. Cresset Press, 1949.

The Achievement of T. S. Eliot by F. O. Matthiessen. Oxford, 1948.

A Reader's Guide to T. S. Eliot by George Williamson. Thames & Hudson, 1955.

Gerard Manley Hopkins by W. H. Gardner. Secker & Warburg, 1948.

The Poetry of Dylan Thomas by Elder Olson. University of Chicago, 1954.

Yeats, the Man and the Masks by Richard Ellmann. Macmillan, 1949.

The Lonely Tower (a study of Yeats) by T. R. Henn. Methuen, 1950.

W. B. Yeats by J. M. Hone. Macmillan, 1942.

The Modern Writer and his World by G. S. Fraser. Andre Deutsch/ Verschoyle, 1954.

New Bearings in English Poetry by F. R. Leavis. Chatto & Windus, 1932. (New Edition, 1950).

The Shaping Spirit (essays on contemporary British and American poets) by A. Alvarez. Chatto & Windus, 1958.

Writers and their Work pamphlets:

    Gerard Manley Hopkins by Geoffrey Grigson.

    W. B. Yeats by G. S. Fraser.

    D. H. Lawrence by Kenneth Young.

    T. S. Eliot by M. C. Bradbrook.

    W. H. Auden by Richard Hoggart.

    C. Day Lewis by Clifford Dyment.

    Dylan Thomas by G. S. Fraser.

    Edwin Muir by J. C. Hall.

    Robert Graves by Martin Seymour-Smith.

2. ANTHOLOGIES

The Faber Book of Modern Verse, edited by Michael Roberts, revised by Anne Ridler. Faber, 1951.

The Faber Book of Twentieth Century Verse, edited by John Heath-Stubbs and David Wright. Faber, 1953.

Poetry Now, edited by G. S. Fraser. Faber, 1956.

Penguin Book of Contemporary Verse, edited by Kenneth Allott. Penguin, 1950.

Oxford Book of Modern Verse, edited by W. B. Yeats. Oxford, 1936.

New Lines, edited by Robert Conquest. Macmillan, 1956.

Mavericks, edited by Howard Sergeant and Dannie Abse. Editions, Poetry and Poverty, 1956.

Poems of the Mid-Century, edited by John Holloway. Harrap, 1957.

Anthologies of contemporary poetry are also published by Dent (Everyman's Library), Chatto & Windus, Heinemann, Methuen, Phoenix House, and several others. The annual P.E.N. anthologies, *New Poems*, are useful; so far there are volumes for 1952–58 inclusive.

3. COLLECTED EDITIONS

W. H. AUDEN: *Collected Shorter Poems 1930–44*, Faber, 1950.

GEORGE BARKER: *Collected Poems*, Faber, 1957.

ROY CAMPBELL: *Collected Poems*, Vol I 1949, Vol. II 1957, John Lane.

T. S. ELIOT: *Collected Poems 1909–35*, Faber, 1936.

WILLIAM EMPSON: *Collected Poems*, Chatto & Windus, 1955.

ROBERT GRAVES: *Collected Poems 1914–47*, Cassell, 1948.

GERARD MANLEY HOPKINS: *Poems*, Oxford, 1948 (3rd revised edition).

D. H. LAWRENCE: *Collected Poems* (three volumes), Heinemann, 1957.

SIDNEY KEYES: *Collected Poems*, Routledge, 1945.

C. DAY LEWIS: *Collected Poems*, Cape, 1954.

EDWIN MUIR: *Collected Poems*, Faber, 1952.

LOUIS MACNEICE: *Collected Poems 1925–48*, Faber, 1949.

WILFRED OWEN: *The Poems*, Chatto & Windus, 1933.

KATHLEEN RAINE: *Collected Poems*, Hamish Hamilton, 1956.
EDITH SITWELL: *The Canticle of the Rose*, 1920–47, Macmillan, 1950.
STEPHEN SPENDER: *Collected Poems, 1928–53*, Faber, 1955.
DYLAN THOMAS: *Collected Poems 1934–52*, Dent, 1952.
W. B. YEATS: *Collected Poems*, Macmillan, 1950.

4. INDIVIDUAL OR UNCOLLECTED BOOKS OF VERSE

DRUMMOND ALLISON: *The Yellow Night*, Fortune Press, 1944.
KINGSLEY AMIS: *A Case of Samples*, Gollancz, 1956.
W. H. AUDEN: *The Orators*, Faber, 1932.
        New Year Letter, Faber, 1941.
        For the Time Being, Faber, 1945.
        The Age of Anxiety, Faber, 1948.
        Nones, Faber, 1952.
        The Shield of Achilles, Faber, 1955.
GEORGE BARKER: *The True Confession of George Barker*, Fore Publications 1950, The Parton Press 1957.
THOMAS BLACKBURN: *In the Fire*, Putnam, 1956.
CHARLES CAUSLEY: *Union Street*, Hart-Davis, 1956.
ROBERT CONQUEST: *Poems*, Macmillan, 1955.
DONALD DAVIE: *Brides of Reason*, Fantasy Press, 1955.
        A Winter Talent, Routledge, 1957.
LAWRENCE DURRELL: *Selected Poems*, Faber, 1956.
T. S. ELIOT: *Four Quartets*, Faber, 1944.
D. J. ENRIGHT: *The Laughing Hyena*, Routledge, 1953.
        Bread Rather Than Blossoms, Secker & Warburg, 1956.
ROY FULLER: *A Lost Season*, Hogarth Press, 1944.
        Counterparts, Verschoyle, 1954.
        Brutus's Orchard, Deutsch, 1957.
DAVID GASCOYNE: *Poems 1937–42*, Poetry London, 1943.
        A Vagrant, John Lehmann, 1950.

ROBERT GRAVES: *Poems and Satires* 1951, Cassell, 1951.
　　　　　　　Poems 1953, Cassell, 1953.
　　　　　　　The Crowning Privilege (contains sixteen new poems), Cassell, 1955.
　　　　　　　Steps (contains twenty-three new poems), Cassell, 1958.

J. C. HALL: *The Summer Dance*, John Lehmann, 1951.

THOM GUNN: *Fighting Terms*, Fantasy Press, 1954.
　　　　　　The Sense of Movement, Faber, 1957.

JOHN HOLLOWAY: *The Minute*, Marvell Press, 1956.

TED HUGHES: *The Hawk in the Rain*, Faber, 1957.

ELIZABETH JENNINGS: *Poems*, Fantasy Press, 1953.
　　　　　　　　　A Way of Looking, Deutsch, 1955.
　　　　　　　　　A Sense of the World, Deutsch, 1958.

PHILIP LARKIN: *The Less Deceived*, Marvell Press, 1955.

ALUN LEWIS: *Raider's Dawn*, Allen & Unwin, 1942.
　　　　　　Ha! Ha! among the Trumpets, Allen & Unwin, 1944.

LOUIS MACNEICE: *Ten Burnt Offerings*, Faber, 1951.
　　　　　　　　Autumn Sequel, Faber, 1954.
　　　　　　　　Visitations, Faber, 1957.

EDWIN MUIR: *One Foot in Eden*, Faber, 1956.

PHILIP OAKES: *Unlucky Jonah*, University of Reading Dept. of Art, 1954.

F. T. PRINCE: *Poems*, Faber, 1938.
　　　　　　　Soldiers Bathing, Fortune Press, 1954.

HENRY REED: *A Map of Verona*, Cape, 1946.

ANNE RIDLER: *The Nine Bright Shiners*, Faber, 1943.
　　　　　　　The Golden Bird, Faber, 1951.

JON SILKIN: *The Peaceable Kingdom*, Chatto & Windus, 1954.
　　　　　　The Two Freedoms, Chatto & Windus, 1958.

JOHN WAIN: *A Word Carved on a Sill*, Routledge, 1956.

5. VERSE DRAMA, ETC.

W. H. AUDEN: *The Dance of Death*, Faber, 1933.

W. H. AUDEN AND CHRISTOPHER ISHERWOOD:
　　　　　　The Dog Beneath the Skin, Faber, 1935.
　　　　　　The Ascent of F.6., Faber, 1936.
　　　　　　On the Frontier, Faber, 1938.

T. S. ELIOT: *The Rock*, Faber, 1934.

Murder in the Cathedral, Faber, 1935 (latest revisions, 1938).

The Family Reunion, Faber, 1939.

The Cocktail Party, Faber, 1950.

The Confidential Clerk, Faber, 1954.

Poetry and Drama, (criticism), Faber, 1951.

The Three Voices of Poetry (criticism), National Book League, 1953.

STEPHEN SPENDER: *Trial of a Judge*, Faber, 1938.

DYLAN THOMAS: *Under Milk Wood*, Dent, 1954.

W. B. YEATS: *Collected Plays*, Macmillan, 1952.

Index

Main references are given in bold type

Acknowledgements

The author and publishers wish to thank the following for the right to quote material in which they hold the copyright in this book:

Mr. T. S. Eliot, Mr. W. H. Auden, Mr. Stephen Spender, Mr. Louis MacNeice, Mr. George Barker, Miss Anne Ridler, Mr. F. T. Prince, Mr. Lawrence Durrell, the late Mr. Edwin Muir, Mr. Thom Gunn and Mr. Ted Hughes (all published by Messrs Faber and Faber Ltd.); Mr. William Empson, Mr. Jon Silkin and the executors of the late Wilfred Owen (all published by Messrs. Chatto and Windus Ltd.); Mr. John Wain, Mr. Donald Davie and Mr. D. J. Enright (all published by Messrs. Routledge and Kegan Paul Ltd.); Mr. Charles Causley and Messrs. Rupert Hart-Davies; Miss Kathleen Raine and Messrs. Hamish Hamilton Ltd.; the executors of Dylan Thomas and Messrs. J. M. Dent and Sons Ltd.; the estate of the late Mrs. Frieda Lawrence for poems by D. H. Lawrence (published by William Heinemann Ltd.); Mr. Robert Graves for extracts from *Collected Poems 1914–1947* (published by Messrs. Cassell and Co. Ltd.); Mrs. W. B. Yeats and Messrs. Macmillan and Co. Ltd. for extracts from *Collected Poems of W. B. Yeats*; The Oxford University Press for extracts from the poetry and prose of G. M. Hopkins; Mr. Philip Larkin and the Marvell Press; Miss Elizabeth Jennings and Mr. Roy Fuller (both published by Messrs. Andre Deutsch); Mr. C. Day Lewis and Mr. Henry Reed (both published by Messrs. Jonathan Cape Ltd.); Mr. Thomas Blackburn (The Hand and Flower Press); Mr. David Gascoyne, and Mr. Geoffrey Hill.

PR
601
T5

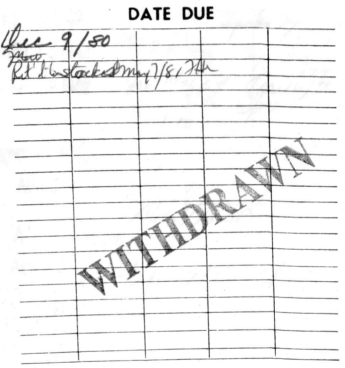